I0078851

The Attachment-Friendly Sleep Plan

For permissions, inquiries, or bulk orders, please contact:
Institute of Sensitive Sleep Consulting
www.instituteofsensitivesleep.com

Printed in Australia

ISBN: 978-1-7642320-2-9

Disclaimer and Waiver of Liability

The information in this book is intended for educational and informational purposes only. It reflects the author's professional knowledge, training, and experience as a mental health professional and founder of the Institute of Sensitive Sleep Consulting. However, this book does not constitute medical, psychological, or legal advice.

Readers are encouraged to use their own professional judgment, seek appropriate supervision, and consult qualified healthcare providers regarding any specific concerns about infant or child health, development, or sleep. The author and publisher disclaim any liability arising directly or indirectly from the use of this material in practice.

Practices around infant sleep may vary across cultures, family values, and individual needs. This book honours that diversity and encourages readers to adapt strategies with care, compassion, and in alignment with current safety guidelines.

Mention of specific methods, techniques, tools, or case examples is for illustration purposes only and does not guarantee specific outcomes.

Contents

With Thanks

* * *

Thanks to Eric and Hannah, who gift me patience, love, purpose.

Welcome to The Attachment-Friendly Sleep Plan

If you're here, there's a good chance you're tired. Really tired. The kind of tired that reshapes how you feel about everything — your child, your partner, your ability to cope, your sense of self.

You may be standing at a difficult crossroads: part of you is desperate for a change, and another part is scared that anything you try will harm the bond you've worked so hard to nurture.

I wrote this book because I've been where you are — both personally and professionally. And I want you to know something right from the beginning:

You can help your baby or child sleep better. You can do it in a way that protects your relationship, not damages it. And you don't have to choose between your child's emotional needs and your own.

There is a path forward that respects both.

Why This Book — and Why Me?

My name is Kel Whittaker, I'm the founder of the Institute of Sensitive Sleep Consulting, an accredited training organisation that has helped educate and certify hundreds of sleep consultants, originating in Australia.

But above that, I'm a mother — one that was exhausted, overwhelmed, and wrestling with the weight of two opposing narratives: one that told me to "just sleep train and get on with it," and another that warned me that if I let my baby cry, I'd damage their developing brain and our attachment.

Neither extreme felt right. And neither explained what to do when my baby just. wouldn't. sleep.

With a background in psychology and social work, I was trained to look beyond quick fixes and understand behaviour within context. I knew sleep was important — for babies, for caregivers, for mental health, for development. But I also knew that many common methods of improving sleep were presented in ways that didn't consider the emotional nuances of parenting.

I wanted something more holistic — an approach that combined the best of behavioural science with the wisdom of attachment theory, and the real-life experience of sleep-deprived parents who want help without harshness.

That's what this book is here to give you.

I did begin my consultancy in Darwin (a regional city in Northern Australia), whilst taking time off from my government job with my first born baby. I was the first Sleep Consultant in Darwin! Pioneering has its perks of course, being the only fish in that pond, however, the flipside is, I was starting from scratch and it was up to me to shape the perception of what this role is and convince people of its benefits. Armed with my studies in Psychology and the weight of sleep deprivation, I was driven to get this right.

I noticed my own sleep problem crept up slowly. Beginning in early adulthood, from around the time I started studying psychology, coincidentally, stress would covertly run my mind, making it more difficult to stay asleep at times. Gradually, it became more of a problem before falling pregnant, and then once I was pregnant, it was a disaster. The threat of not being able to take sleeping pills "in case of emergency" due to the health risk to the pregnancy, meant I was more on edge concerning sleep. On top of that, I was preparing for the impending doom of sleepless nights looking after the baby. Of course pregnancy itself also messes up sleep for even the best sleeper. The days following my son's birth are a blur. I had a 30 hour labour, so zero sleep before birth and then it was near impossible to sleep with all the afterbirth hormones and regular feeding to be done. Visitors would seem to arrive right when I was about to rest. I felt myself about to pass out at one stage, all I could do was eat some cake to stop from fainting in front of well-meaning visitors. The sounds of the hospital were grating me. I could hear every clang and bang in the halls, around the clock. I remember asking a nurse, 'Do people die from sleep deprivation? And if I can't get any sleep, will resting with my eyes closed be good enough?" I longed to be released from hospital, to come back to the comfort and security of my own bed. I was supposed to stay 5 nights but I self-discharged on the fourth. The night we returned home with baby, I had just finally settled him and hopped into bed for a few minutes, finally about to catch some shut-eye, when the door bell rang. A stranger at the door in her underwear, pleading to use the phone. We obliged of course, gave her my clothes and offered to take her anywhere. Why tonight.

In the first six weeks, a nurse commented on how alert my son was. I thought it was a compliment that he was super bright for his age. I soon realized that it was not normal for a newborn to be awake for hours, and slowly my obsession with finding the magic code to unlock sleep started to grow. After much research and on the verge of flying a famous sleep consultant up to Darwin, my passion for this business was born. I can do this. After resolving my son's sleep, parenthood was bliss. Too blissful, that we thought we needed the challenge of a sibling. At the end of the same year as giving birth to my first, I fell pregnant again. My first clue was morning sickness on Christmas Day.

I studied sleep consulting with several American providers and leaped into my new career, working around caring for my baby. I enjoyed the thrill of helping others and getting results, so much so, that I did not stop when I was heavily pregnant with my second baby, and soon after she was born, I remember taking her with me to consults, breastfeeding on a client's sofa as we talked. Something changed though, the more I learned about parenting through my own experiences, and the differences between the siblings, the more I thought there must be other methods to helping babies sleep, than the cookie-cutter strategies.

I listened to parents' views on co-sleeping and their bonds through breastfeeding. I revisited my old text books on attachment theory, and dug deep into learning about attachment parenting until the penny dropped. There was a huge gap in this industry for approaches that were effective (evidence informed) yet sensitive to the emotions felt by parents, the mental wellbeing of infants and protecting the attachment bond between care-giver and child. Medical and allied health professionals were only educated on standardized and simplified strategies. I know, as I also enrolled and underwent the university training module offered to family doctors. It took less than 3 hours.

And so the Institute of Sensitive Sleep Consulting was born. Our first program was developed and approved whilst I was completing my Masters qualification. I had six students in my pilot intake. The program was well-received and within a few years, it had started an industry movement, with many other providers adding a gentle flavor to their courses. Whilst I was not the first to bring gentle methods into the spotlight, I was the first to marry the psychology of attachment theory with evidence informed sleep interventions and behavioral principles of psychology. Fundamentally, with this approach, we are able to adapt any sleep training intervention into a plan that respects the bond and wellbeing of both child and parent. The majority of sleep disorders in children are behavioral, therefore, it is vital that training is crafted from a behavioral science perspective. Of course, we have vast input from related professions such as nursing, midwifery and early childhood education, nutrition, and even pediatric osteopathy, which add tremendous value to a holistic approach.

What Makes This Book Different?

This isn't a "sleep training book." But I'm not here to demonise sleep training, either.

Instead, I'll guide you through a ladder of sleep support that:

- Starts with the foundations (environment, routines, rhythm)

- Moves through gentle, responsive techniques (like presence and fading)

- Introduces behavioural interventions (yes, even versions of "sleep training") that are respectful, flexible, and emotionally safe

Because the truth is, structure and sensitivity can co-exist. You can hold your child with warmth and still hold a boundary. You can offer emotional availability and still change habits. You can teach sleep... without breaking the bond.

How to Use This Book

Each chapter is designed to equip you — not overwhelm you.

I'll walk you through:

- What's biologically normal in baby and child sleep

- How to know when help is needed

- What behavioural strategies are available

- How to implement change step-by-step, in a way that feels right for your child and your values

Whether your child is four months or five years old, whether you bedshare or bottle-feed or both, there is something in this book for you. And you won't find judgment here. Only information, options, and support.

A Final Word Before We Begin…

You may have been made to feel like helping your child sleep better is selfish. Or that doing nothing is what good parents do. But you matter too. And rest is a form of care — for you, and for the child you love.

If you're ready to find a way forward that feels aligned with both science and sensitivity, I'm honoured to walk with you.

Let's begin.

Chapter 1: What Babies Are Meant to Do

Understanding Developmental Sleep (and Why You're Not Doing It Wrong)

If you've ever Googled "how much sleep should my baby be getting?" or "is it normal for my toddler to wake up every night?" — you're not alone. In fact, you're among thousands of parents each day typing those exact questions, often with a baby in one arm and a half-drunk cup of tea in the other.

Sleep is one of the most common — and confusing — struggles in early parenthood. It's also one of the most misunderstood. Because so much of what we expect from our children around sleep... isn't actually developmentally normal.

Let's start by clearing the air.

You are not failing. Your child is not broken. And sleep, as it turns out, is not a linear milestone — it's a relationship, a rhythm, and a skill that grows with time, support, and understanding.

What Does "Normal" Sleep Look Like?

It's a simple question, but the answer depends on who you ask. A sleep-deprived parent might say, "A baby that sleeps through the night." A grandparent might recall, "You were sleeping twelve hours by the time you were three weeks old." A popular parenting blog might insist that all babies *can* sleep through the night by three months, and if they're not, it's because you're doing something wrong.

Let's replace expectation with education.

In truth, normal infant sleep is:

- **Fragmented**: Babies cycle through light and deep sleep more often than adults

- **Variable**: Some nights they wake twice, some nights five times — even without a clear reason

- **Responsive**: Babies rouse in response to hunger, discomfort, developmental leaps, and simply the need for proximity

It's also important to note that night waking is not just common — it's protective. Waking up regularly in the early months supports breastfeeding, reduces the risk of SIDS, and ensures needs are met as babies grow rapidly.

Still, normal doesn't mean *sustainable*. While frequent waking is expected in early infancy, many families need support when sleep disruption becomes chronic or distressing — and that's okay. Wanting more sleep does not mean you're impatient or unloving. It means you're human.

Sleep Isn't a Milestone — It's a Maturation Process

We often think of sleep like walking or talking — a skill to be "achieved." But that's a misrepresentation. Sleep is a **neurological process**, influenced by biology, temperament, environment, and experience. Like all developmental changes, it doesn't unfold in a straight line.

Consider these developmental truths:

- Newborns have no concept of "night" and "day." Their circadian rhythms (internal clocks) don't start developing until around 6–8 weeks of age.

- Around 4 months, babies experience a biological "sleep reorganisation" that leads to lighter, more adult-like sleep cycles — and often, more frequent waking.

- Teething, illness, growth spurts, and brain development can all disrupt sleep — sometimes without warning or explanation.

- Even toddlers and preschoolers may struggle with staying asleep, night fears, or early rising well into age 3–5.

So if your baby once slept for a stretch and now wakes frequently, or your toddler who "used to be fine" is now calling out at midnight, that's not regression. That's progression — it's growth showing up in sleep.

The Sleep Cycle: Why "Sleeping Through the Night" Doesn't Mean Zero Wakes

It's time to bust one of the biggest myths in parenting:

> **"Sleeping through the night" means never waking up.**

Actually, all humans — infants, children, adults — **wake briefly** multiple times during the night as we move through **natural sleep cycles**.

These cycles alternate between:

- **Non-REM (deep) sleep** and

- **REM (light/dream) sleep**

And with each shift between these stages, our brain briefly **"checks in"** with the body and environment. This is a completely **normal, protective function** — a kind of internal survival mechanism.

Why We Wake Briefly

During these **light arousals**, our body is asking: *"Am I too hot or cold?"* *"What was that noise?"* *"Do I need to move?"* *"Am I safe?"*

Healthy sleepers don't usually remember these moments. We might roll over, adjust the blanket, or shift positions — and drift right back to sleep.

Adults with **insomnia** or disrupted sleep (due to stress, pain, alcohol, or anxiety) often become **hyper-aware** of these arousals. Once awake, they may fixate on it: *"Why am I awake again?"* *"What time is it?"* *"Now I'll be wrecked tomorrow…"*

This mental spiral makes returning to sleep much harder. Some even resort to coping mechanisms —

reading, cleaning, turning on screens — to pass the time.

What This Means for Babies and Toddlers

Babies, too, go through these natural sleep cycles. But if they're not yet **self-settling** or if something in their environment changes (e.g. lighting, sound, smell, physical discomfort), they may wake fully and call out for help.

So, no, your baby will never literally sleep 8–12 hours without *ever* waking.
 But yes, they can learn to return to sleep more easily — especially if:

- Their environment is consistent

- Their sleep associations are flexible

- Their body is regulated and ready for rest

Using the Sleep Phases Chart

A helpful visual tool is the **Sleep Phases Overnight chart** (see next page for reference). This chart depicts the average sleep architecture of a child across a night — showing how we start the night in deeper sleep and progressively cycle through lighter stages as the night goes on.

Key observations:

- **Deepest sleep happens early** in the night (before midnight)

- **Lighter, more fragmented sleep** occurs in the early morning hours

- One final opportunity for **deep sleep** may happen just before wake-up

This chart is a great educational tool when working with families. It shows that:

- It's **normal** to wake multiple times a night

- Most wakings are **non-problematic** — unless they become distressing or prolonged

- Children can learn to move through these phases more smoothly with the right support

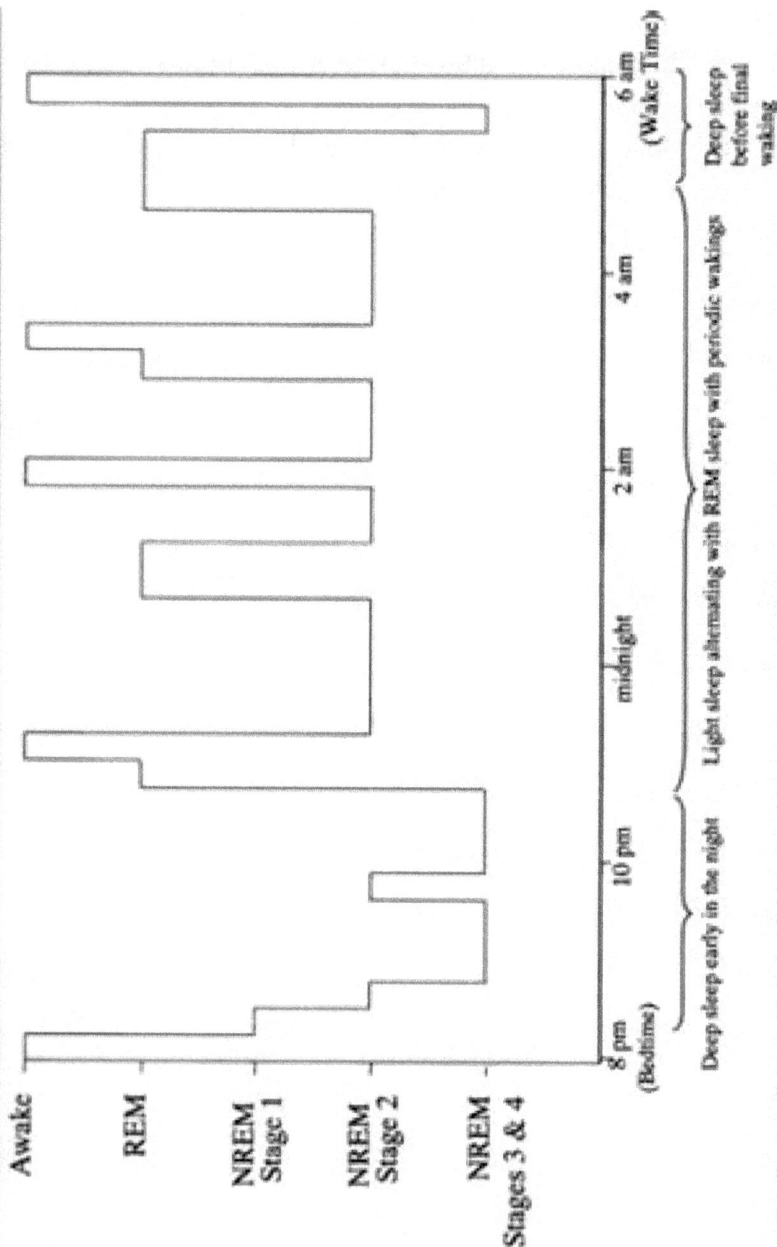

Medscape   www.medscape.com

Awake

REM

NREM
Stage 1

NREM
Stage 2

NREM
Stages 3 & 4

8 pm   10 pm   midnight   2 am   4 am   6 am
(Bedtime)   (Wake Time)

Deep sleep early in the night   Light sleep alternating with REM sleep with periodic wakings   Deep sleep before final waking

Source: J Pediatr Health Care @ 2004 Mosby, Inc.

Common Questions Parents Ask — and What the Chart Can Tell Us

"Why does my baby wake every night about 45–60 minutes after bedtime?"

This is often when they're moving from light sleep into their **first deep sleep phase** — a common transition point where some children struggle to resettle. It may suggest that:

- The sleep environment has changed (noise, light)

- There's discomfort or digestion interference

- They haven't yet developed **self-settling** skills

"Why does my toddler wake up at 5 a.m. and can't go back to sleep?"

This is when both body temperature and sleep depth are at their lowest — making it harder to resettle, especially if they're light sleepers or overtired. Keeping the early morning environment dark and warm may help.

"We tiptoe after bedtime, but she still wakes when the dishwasher starts…"
If your child needs *silence* to fall asleep but the environment gets noisier as the evening goes on, the shift may feel jarring during sleep transitions. The goal is to keep **consistent background conditions** — soft white noise can help.

Practical Takeaways

- **Don't panic about night wakings** — they're biologically normal.

- **Sleep regulation is about how quickly and easily a child returns to sleep**, not about never waking.

- If a baby can't return to sleep without help every time, it might be time to gently build skills using the strategies we'll explore in later chapters.

- **Early morning wakes** may be related to body temperature drops, overstimulation, overtiredness, or a mistimed nap routine.

- Use tools like the **Sleep Phases chart** to help families understand what's biologically expected — and what can be changed with gentle, responsive interventions.

The Trouble with "Self-Soothing"

One of the most misunderstood terms in modern parenting is "self-soothing." You've probably heard or read that babies need to learn to self-soothe in order to sleep through the night. But let's unpack what this really means.

True self-soothing — the ability to calm oneself after distress — is not a skill babies are born with. It develops gradually through **co-regulation**. In other words, babies learn to soothe by being soothed.

Here's what the research and child development theory tells us:

- Infants are biologically wired to seek comfort from a caregiver when distressed

- Their stress-response systems are immature and rely on **external regulation** (your voice, your touch, your presence)

- Over time, with consistent, attuned care, they internalise these experiences — and that's how they build their own ability to regulate emotions

So when a baby cries at 2 a.m. and you pick them up, rock them, or simply sit beside them with a hand on their chest — you're not "spoiling" them. You're shaping their brain toward trust, emotional resilience, and yes... eventually, independent sleep.

Self-Settling vs. Self-Soothing: What's the Difference?

You may have heard these terms used interchangeably — "self-soothing" and "self-settling" — but they're not the same. Understanding the difference is crucial when we're talking about babies, stress, and sleep.

Self-soothing refers to a person's ability to regulate their own emotions — to come down from a heightened state of distress or upset without external support. This is a *social-emotional skill*, one that develops gradually over years and depends heavily on secure attachment and repeated experiences of co-regulation.

By contrast, **self-settling** refers to the physiological process of falling asleep — the ability to *transition from a wakeful state into sleep*, without help like feeding, rocking, patting, or being held. This isn't about emotion as much as it's about **neurology** and **habit**.

Even in very young infants, the body has the capacity to drift into sleep when tired and conditions are optimal — darkened room, full tummy, low stimulation. While babies may not be able to "soothe themselves" from stress or fear, some can, at times, fall asleep independently when calm and content.

Put simply:

- **Self-soothing** = calming yourself down emotionally

- **Self-settling** = being able to fall asleep without external help

Both are important, but they develop on different timelines and serve different functions.

What Polyvagal Theory Adds to This Understanding

Dr Stephen Porges' **Polyvagal Theory** gives us a powerful lens to understand what's happening in a child's nervous system during sleep — and why co-regulation is so crucial for young infants.

According to Porges, our nervous system has three main states:

1. **Ventral vagal**: Calm, connected, socially engaged (optimal state for learning and resting)

2. **Sympathetic**: Fight or flight (mobilised, agitated, alert)

3. **Dorsal vagal**: Freeze or shutdown (withdrawn, dissociated, collapsed)

For sleep to occur, a child's nervous system must be in the **ventral vagal** state — calm and safe enough to allow the body to relax and drift into sleep.

But here's the key insight:
Infants and toddlers don't get there on their own.

They *borrow regulation* from their caregivers through:

- Physical proximity

- Soothing voice tone

- Predictable routines

- Touch, warmth, and rhythm

This is co-regulation — and it teaches the body that rest is safe.

Over time, with consistent support, the child's brain develops the ability to **shift into the ventral vagal state independently**. That's when self-settling starts to become more consistent. But if a child is left in a distressed sympathetic state (crying, unsettled), the nervous system stays activated — making it harder, not easier, to fall asleep or learn new sleep habits.

What does this mean practically?

It means:

- A baby can learn to self-settle, but needs co-regulation to get there

- Emotional safety isn't a barrier to sleep training — it's the foundation

- Crying alone doesn't build independence — it risks dysregulation

- Sleep plans that ignore the nervous system are unlikely to succeed (at least not without cost)

When we talk about behavioural sleep support in this book, it's always within this biological and relational framework.

We're not just trying to make sleep happen. We're supporting the nervous system to feel safe enough *for* sleep to happen.

Your Baby Isn't Manipulating You

One of the most harmful myths that circulates in early parenting circles is the idea that babies cry "for attention" — and that responding reinforces negative behaviour. But babies don't cry to manipulate. They cry to communicate.

When a baby cries at bedtime, it may be because:

- They're hungry

- They're overtired

- They need help transitioning from wake to sleep

- They're in discomfort or pain

- They want to be close to their caregiver

Sometimes, even if all needs are met, babies still cry as a form of release — a way of working through their overstimulated nervous system.

Responding to your baby doesn't mean they'll "never learn." It means they'll learn that sleep is safe, and that they're not alone. And from that place of trust, we can gently introduce new sleep habits that work for everyone.

If you've spent more than five minutes in a parent Facebook group, you've probably noticed that "sleep training" is the parenting world's equivalent of pineapple on pizza — either people love it or they think it's an unspeakable crime against humanity. And like most polarising topics, the truth is far more nuanced than either camp admits.

I want to strip away the noise and help you understand what sleep training actually is, what the research says, and — most importantly — how to interpret that research through the lens of your own child and your own parenting values. My goal isn't to convince you to use a particular method, but to equip you to make a decision you can feel confident in.

What Sleep Training Actually Means

In its broadest sense, "sleep training" is any process where parents intentionally change the way their child falls asleep or stays asleep — often by reducing how much help the child receives from a parent during the night. This could be as simple as pausing before you pick up your baby, or as structured as following a minute-by-minute plan.

Some people think "sleep training" automatically means leaving a baby to cry alone. Others imagine it's a complicated, military-style schedule involving stopwatches and clipboards. But in reality, sleep training is a spectrum — from the most gradual, hands-on changes to more direct behavioural interventions.

The goal of sleep training is usually to help a child learn to fall asleep independently, so that when they wake in the night (as all humans do), they can resettle without needing a parent every time. The *way* this is done — and the emotional climate in which it's done — matters just as much as the end result.

Why the Topic is So Polarising

For many parents, the phrase "sleep training" brings up strong feelings because it touches on two very personal things:

1. How we respond to our child's needs

2. What kind of parents we want to be

Those on one side of the debate worry that certain methods — particularly those involving crying without immediate comfort — could harm attachment or cause emotional distress. Those on the other side often point out that a chronically sleep-deprived family can't function well, and that independent sleep skills can be taught in ways that are safe and respectful.

Both perspectives have truth in them. And this is where we have to move past the all-or-nothing thinking and ask: *How do we support sleep in a way that's developmentally realistic, emotionally safe, and sustainable for the whole family?*

What the Research Says — and Doesn't Say

You'll often hear sweeping statements like "research proves sleep training doesn't harm babies" or "science shows controlled crying damages attachment." Neither statement is accurate without a lot of footnotes.

Here's what we actually know from the research so far:

- Short-term outcomes: Studies show that behavioural sleep interventions (including controlled comforting and "camping out" approaches) can reduce night wakings and help parents feel more rested, often within a couple of weeks. These effects tend to be strongest when the plan is followed consistently.

- Long-term outcomes: Most follow-up studies find no significant differences in children's attachment security, emotional wellbeing, or behaviour between families who used certain forms of sleep training and those who didn't. However — and this is important — the research almost always focuses on *average outcomes*. That means it can miss the experiences of children who don't cope well with certain approaches.

- Limitations: Many studies have small sample sizes, don't account for temperament differences, and don't track the quality of parental responsiveness during sleep training. So when you read "no harm found," it doesn't necessarily mean *no harm is possible*. It means harm wasn't detected in that particular group under those particular conditions.

The Missing Context

One of the biggest gaps in the "sleep training" conversation is the role of how it's done. The difference between a parent who leaves a baby to cry alone in a dark room for hours and one who uses a gradual, responsive approach with consistent reassurance is enormous — yet both may be labelled "sleep training" in research.

This means parents can't just copy a study's conclusion and expect the same results. You have to consider:

- Your child's temperament

- Their developmental stage

- Your own emotional bandwidth

- How you'll respond to distress in the process

In my years of working with families, I've seen gentle, attachment-friendly sleep training transform the lives of exhausted parents without leaving a scratch on the parent-child bond. I've also seen situations where the exact same method felt overwhelming for a sensitive child or triggered deep parental guilt.

One mum I worked with, Sarah, was sure she'd never use a method involving any crying. But after months of broken sleep and rising anxiety, she chose a gradual "check-and-comfort" approach. The crying that did happen was short, supported, and always responded to. Within a week, her baby was sleeping longer stretches, and Sarah felt calmer and more present in the day.

On the flip side, another family came to me after they tried a controlled crying method on their spirited toddler. Even with short check-ins, the child became more clingy during the day and bedtime battles escalated. I helped craft a slower, more hands-on method, and progress was slower but far gentler.

The takeaway? It's not about picking the "right" method from a chart. It's about finding the method that's the right fit for your *child* — and for you.

Can We Talk About Controlled Crying?

Understanding Graduated Extinction in Light of Attachment and Self-Regulation

Let's talk honestly about one of the most controversial methods in infant sleep support: **controlled crying**, also known as **graduated extinction**.

At face value, the method sounds simple:

- You put the child down awake

- Leave the room for a set amount of time

- Return briefly to reassure

- Gradually extend the time between check-ins over several nights

It's a structured behavioural intervention designed to reduce parent-led settling (like feeding or rocking) and to help the child fall asleep independently.

And here's the truth: **controlled crying can be effective**.

Research consistently shows that:

- Graduated extinction reduces sleep onset latency (how long it takes to fall asleep)

- It decreases night wakings for many families

- It does not cause long-term harm in most children who are otherwise well-supported and securely attached

But — and this is where nuance matters — **how** the method is used, **when**, and **with what level of attunement** can significantly affect how a child experiences it.

Crying Alone vs. Structured Support

Earlier we discussed the nervous system states described in **Polyvagal Theory**. To return to that framework, we know that:

- A child needs to be in a regulated (ventral vagal) state to fall asleep

- Prolonged, unsupported crying keeps the child in a sympathetic (fight-or-flight) state

- If they cry long enough without resolution, they may drop into dorsal vagal shutdown (freeze/collapse)

From the outside, this may *look* like the child has "settled." But physiologically, they may have simply **disengaged** due to overwhelm — not found calm, but gone still.

This is why you'll often hear the phrase:

> **"Crying alone doesn't build independence — it risks dysregulation."**

And it's true. **When controlled crying is misapplied —** without preparation, without emotional context, or in very young or highly sensitive children — it can backfire. Not because the strategy is inherently cruel, but because it disregards the child's physiological state and need for co-regulation.

So Why Does Controlled Crying *Work*?

When used appropriately, with children developmentally ready to **self-settle**, and with **structured reassurance** and a regulated environment, graduated extinction can help a child:

- Practice the physiological skill of falling asleep independently

- Develop predictable expectations around bedtime

- Reduce reliance on external sleep associations (like rocking or feeding)

It works **not** because the crying itself "teaches" the child anything — but because the consistent, low-stimulation environment **supports self-settling**, and the child adapts to falling asleep in those conditions.

In these situations, crying is often a protest — an expression of change, not trauma. With proper parental regulation, responsive check-ins, and daytime emotional availability, many children experience this kind of plan not as abandonment, but as a **clear, calm shift in sleep patterns**.

What This Book Teaches Instead

I do not promote cry-it-out in its full extinction form (no check-ins, no contact) — especially for young babies.

But I *do* teach sleep plans that:

- Create a safe, regulated environment

- Involve gradual reduction in hands-on help (fading)

- Offer repeated reassurance without over-stimulating

- Recognise that tears may still happen — but they are *heard*, *understood*, and *held*

This might look like:

- Sitting by the cot with a hand on your child's body as they learn to fall asleep

- Responding to crying with calm presence, but not automatically picking up

- Stretching out response times by seconds, not minutes, in a way that matches your child's regulation capacity

- Letting your child express emotion *with* you, not *in spite of* you

The Bottom Line

Crying itself is not harmful. What matters is the **meaning** of the crying, and the **context** in which it occurs.

If your child is:

- In a safe, secure attachment relationship

- Emotionally held throughout the day

- Offered predictable routines and cues

- Given opportunities for self-settling in a calm and attuned way

… then occasional protest at bedtime is not only okay — it's expected.

But if your child is:

- Very young or highly dysregulated

- Crying for long stretches without support

- Left alone in distress without responsive care

… then the same method can contribute to **nervous system dysregulation**, **sleep aversion**, or **emotional insecurity**.

This is why behavioural interventions **must be tailored**. They are not inherently damaging, nor inherently gentle. It depends on **how** and **why** they are used — and **who** is using them.

In the chapters to come, I'll guide you in creating a sleep support plan that:

- Respects your child's biology and temperament

- Aligns with your parenting values

- Leaves room for connection, structure, and rest — for everyone

Because when used wisely, behavioural strategies can be part of a gentle, attachment-friendly path.

Sleep Is a Relationship

One of the biggest shifts I hope this book brings is in how we think about sleep — not as a behaviour to fix, but as a **relationship to support**.

Think of sleep as a dance between biology, environment, and connection:

- Biology: the natural rhythm and readiness of your child's body

- Environment: the sensory and emotional conditions in which sleep occurs

- Connection: the emotional safety that makes it possible to let go and rest

When sleep is challenging, it's tempting to focus on the behaviour. But behaviour is the surface. Underneath, there's always a reason — and often, a need.

By recognising that sleep is relational, we begin to focus less on control, and more on **support**. We ask:

- What does my child need in order to feel safe enough to sleep?

- What might be getting in the way of their natural ability to rest?

- How can I create a rhythm that respects both their development and my needs?

This is not about letting children "rule the house." It's about leading with connection so that structure can land safely.

You Can Trust Your Instincts — and Still Ask for Help

In the current parenting climate, it often feels like we're expected to choose a side: instinct vs. strategy, love vs. limits, baby-led vs. parent-led. But the truth is far more nuanced.

It's entirely possible — and deeply beneficial — to:

- Honour your intuition *and* learn from science

- Comfort your child *and* set boundaries

- Be emotionally present *and* change routines that aren't working

This is where attachment-informed behavioural support lives. And it's where this book will meet you.

Parent Reflection:

This reflection is an invitation to get honest — and curious — about the beliefs and emotions you bring into your child's sleep. There are no right or wrong answers, only what's true for you right now.

How do I feel when my child cries at bedtime (or during the night)?

What does it bring up in me — fear, sadness, guilt, frustration, urgency?

Where did I learn those responses to crying? Are they shaped by how I was parented, or by what I've read or been told?

What do I believe about "independence" when it comes to baby sleep?

Have I ever felt pressure to push it too early? What does independence really mean to me?

When I imagine my child learning to fall asleep on their own, what do I hope they feel?

Calm? Safe? Confident? What can I do to support those feelings, even if some tears are part of the process?

What would it feel like to trust that crying is not always harm — and that I can hold space for both growth and comfort?

What You Can Expect Next

In the chapters to come, we'll introduce the **Ladder of Sleep Support** — a flexible, compassionate framework that offers multiple entry points depending on your child's age, temperament, and your family's needs.

But before we get to techniques and plans, we'll explore the **emotional and cultural pressures** that make sleep such a fraught topic — and why it's not just about your baby.

Because to truly support sleep, we have to understand how it makes us feel as parents too.

Let's keep going.

Chapter 2: Why Sleep Feels So Hard

The Emotional Toll on Parents, and the Myths That Make It Worse

Sleep — or more accurately, the lack of it — touches every part of our parenting experience. It affects how we bond, how we function, how we feel about ourselves. And when it's not working, it has a way of making everything else harder.

It's not just that your baby isn't sleeping. It's that suddenly, you don't know if *you're allowed* to feel overwhelmed by it. It's that you've read six different books and they all contradict each other. It's that your mother says you're spoiling the baby, while your friend says to just wait it out. It's the creeping guilt that maybe your child is struggling because of *something you've done*.

So let's pause and take this chapter to name something that doesn't get said enough:

You're not failing. And you're not alone in feeling like sleep should be easier than it is.

Why Sleep Feels So Loaded

When you bring your baby home from the hospital, one of the first questions people ask you is, "Are they sleeping well?"

The assumption is that good babies sleep, and competent parents get them there quickly. This seemingly innocent question can carry a subtle (and often unintended) message:

> "If your child isn't sleeping, something must be wrong."

It taps into a deep vulnerability. Because sleep is one of the first measurable rhythms of life with a baby, it becomes a proxy for how well we think we're doing as parents. If sleep isn't going well, it can feel like a direct reflection of our competence, our consistency, or our ability to cope.

In reality, sleep is a dynamic process influenced by dozens of variables:

- Age and developmental stage

- Temperament and sensory processing

- Feeding method and frequency

- Parental availability, mental health, and environment

And it's *normal* for it to be inconsistent.

The Guilt Gap

When sleep becomes a struggle, guilt often follows closely behind — regardless of what choices you make.

If you try to follow attachment parenting advice, you might feel guilty for craving space or disliking night waking. If you try a sleep training method, you might feel guilty for allowing crying, even in a structured and supported way. If you choose to co-sleep, you might feel judged for not "encouraging independence."

If you move toward more independence, you might worry you're missing emotional cues.

In short: you can feel guilty no matter what you do.

This is what we call the **guilt gap** — the emotional chasm between what we believe we *should* be doing, and what we're *actually* doing in the trenches of sleep deprivation.

But let me offer this gentle truth:

> Guilt is not a reliable measure of whether something is right or wrong.
> It's often a measure of how conflicted we feel between competing messages.

The Impact of Cultural Messaging

Modern parents are surrounded by mixed messages:

- "Follow your baby's cues."

- "Don't create bad habits."

- "Be responsive."

- "Encourage independence."

- "Trust your instincts."

- "Stick to a routine."

You may hear:

- "You're the expert on your baby's needs."

- Followed by: "You'll ruin them if you don't do it right."

Sleep advice often swings between extremes:

- One camp advocates total responsiveness: feed, rock, hold — no limits, no expectations.

- Another insists that boundaries must be taught early, and that babies are capable of "manipulating" sleep routines from just a few months old.

This leaves little room for the in-between — for nuanced, flexible, attachment-informed approaches that combine structure and sensitivity.

That's where this book comes in.

The Hidden Grief of Lost Sleep

Sleep loss isn't just physically depleting. It carries a kind of emotional grief that's difficult to name. You grieve:

- The parts of your identity that feel blurry in the fog of exhaustion

- The time with your partner that's been lost to tag-team nights

- The sense of control and predictability that used to shape your life

- The idea that rest should be a given, not a luxury

Sleep loss touches your memory, your mood, your confidence, and your ability to regulate your own emotions. When you're up four times a night, even basic decisions — like what to eat or how to respond to your toddler — can feel impossibly complex.

It's important to acknowledge this. Because until you name the weight of sleep deprivation, it's hard to know where it's leaking into the rest of your life.

And once you name it, you can begin to approach sleep support not as an act of desperation, but as an act of care.

Why Crying Affects Us So Deeply

Another reason sleep feels so difficult — particularly when it involves any crying — is that humans are biologically wired to respond to a baby's distress.

Crying is a primal signal. It alerts us to potential danger, unmet needs, or pain. When your child cries, it activates your **stress response** — sometimes even before your brain has had time to interpret what's happening.

And when that crying continues, or when you're unsure how to respond, it can feel like you're choosing between:

- Letting your child cry (and fearing long-term harm), or

- Abandoning your own sleep, health, or wellbeing

That's a false choice. And it's not sustainable.

This book will show you a third option:

Creating a plan that honours the biology of sleep and the biology of attachment. One that allows for protest, but never for emotional abandonment. One where tears are heard, held, and supported — even when they're part of change.

When "Normal" Doesn't Feel Okay

Sometimes parents hear: "It's normal for babies to wake frequently" — and that's true. But what's also true is that **normal doesn't mean tolerable.**

You can accept that night waking is developmentally expected *and* feel ready for a change.

You're allowed to say:

- "I know this is biologically appropriate, but I need more rest."

- "I love my child deeply, and I'm not coping with sleep the way it is."

- "I want to support my child's emotions and also support my own needs."

You can be a responsive parent who still wants a sleep plan.

That is not selfish. That is sustainable.

A Note on Mental Health

Before we move on, I want to gently acknowledge something else: for many parents, sleep disruption triggers or worsens symptoms of **anxiety**, **postnatal depression**, **irritability**, or **burnout**.

Sleep is not a luxury — it is a mental health intervention.

If you are feeling hopeless, constantly on edge, or emotionally numb, know that this book may help with sleep, but you might also need additional support. There is no shame in that.

Getting help is not weakness. It's parenting with strength and clarity.

Sleep difficulties in young children don't just affect children — they affect entire households. And most acutely, they affect mothers. Research shows that mothers of infants and toddlers with sleep problems are significantly more likely to experience:

- Symptoms of **postnatal depression and anxiety**

- Sleep disturbances of their own

- Increased stress and reduced coping capacity

- Feelings of guilt, failure, or hopelessness

- A disrupted sense of self and identity

In many ways, *the way your child sleeps becomes the climate in which you mother*. That's why this book isn't just about sleep — it's about **emotional safety for everyone**, including you.

But Where Do You Start?

Should you work on your baby's sleep... or your own stress first?

This is a common dilemma. You're exhausted and mentally overloaded, but you worry that trying to change anything (like sleep patterns) will make things worse before they get better.

Here's a framework to help decide where to focus:

Start with sleep support if:

- You feel relatively stable during the day, but nights are your biggest challenge

- You notice your child is overtired, cranky, or struggling with routines

- You've got the mental bandwidth to try something new (even slowly)

- You have some support — a partner, friend, or sleep plan to guide you

Start with your own mental health if:

- You feel overwhelmed most of the time, even during the day

- You feel numb, detached, teary, or irritable — especially without clear reason

- You're experiencing panic, dread, intrusive thoughts, or excessive guilt

- The idea of making even small changes to your child's routine feels paralysing

There's no wrong place to begin. But there's one key idea I want you to take with you:

> Your sleep matters too. Your wellbeing is not an afterthought — it's foundational.

Let me tell you a story — one I've heard in many forms over the years. It's not about one mum, but many. Maybe you'll see a bit of yourself in it.

"I'm not sure if the problem is her sleep... or mine," the mum said, her eyes full but her voice steady, as if she was afraid it would crack if she softened.

Her baby, 10 months old, had just started sleeping in longer chunks. By all accounts, things were *getting better*. But mum wasn't feeling better. In fact, she was feeling worse.

"Now that I can sleep," she whispered, *"I can't."*

She was lying awake for hours after bedtime, scrolling, rechecking the monitor, mentally rehearsing the next feed, the next cry, the next what-if. Even when her daughter slept soundly, *she didn't trust it* — and her body never quite let go.

We talked about how stress, anxiety, and even trauma can reshape the nervous system. When you've spent months (or years) in a state of high alert, your brain doesn't suddenly switch off the moment your baby does. It takes time — and often support — to downshift.

We made a plan that wasn't just about baby sleep. It included:

- A calming bedtime routine for *mum*, not just baby

- Turning off the monitor and letting her partner be the "default responder" some nights

- Identifying the "good enough" signs that her daughter was safe and okay

- And recognising that postnatal sleep issues aren't always about the baby

The biggest shift came when she gave herself permission to say:
 "Even if my baby is sleeping through... I'm still allowed to need help."

This isn't uncommon. Even when baby sleep improves, some parents stay stuck in "survival mode." Sleep is a physical process — but it's also a psychological one. And when the mind has been on high alert for months, it can take time to feel safe enough to rest.

Could I Have Postnatal Anxiety or Depression?

If you're wondering whether what you're feeling is "normal new mum stress" or something more, here are some signs that may indicate **postnatal depression or anxiety**:

You might notice:

- Trouble sleeping even when the baby sleeps

- Racing thoughts or constant worry

- Feeling flat, hopeless, or emotionally detached

- Tearfulness that feels overwhelming

- Feeling like you're going through the motions

- Irritability or anger that feels hard to control

- Difficulty enjoying your baby, partner, or anything at all

- Physical symptoms like fatigue, nausea, tight chest, or headaches

- Thoughts like "I can't do this" or "They'd be better off without me"

These are not signs of weakness — they are signs of exhausted nervous systems and depleted reserves. And they are more common than most people realise. An estimated 1 in 5 mothers experience postnatal depression, and many more experience anxiety that goes unrecognised.

If anything here feels familiar, you are not alone. Support is available — from GPs, psychologists, perinatal services, peer groups, or even specialised sleep consultants with a mental health lens.

Getting help is not a luxury. It's a protective step — for you, your child, and your family's wellbeing.

What Protects Mothers From Sleep-Related Burnout?

There's no formula for preventing mental health challenges entirely — especially when sleep deprivation is ongoing. But certain **protective factors** can make a big difference in how well mothers cope, even during hard seasons.

These include:

1. Predictability (Even If It's Imperfect)
Having some sense of when rest will happen (nap windows, bedtime routine, even a partner's availability) helps reduce overwhelm. Chaos is hard on the brain. Rhythm helps us feel grounded.

2. Social Support
Being able to talk honestly with someone who won't judge — a partner, friend, professional, or peer group — dramatically reduces emotional load. Connection is medicine.

3. Permission to Rest
Even short rests matter. A 20-minute lie down. A skipped chore. Letting go of the idea that you must "earn" rest by ticking every box.

4. Self-Compassion
The voice in your head matters. The more you speak to yourself with warmth ("this is hard, but I'm doing my best"), the better your brain tolerates stress.

5. Low-Stimulation Evenings
Screens, bright lights, and busy tasks late at night confuse the body clock. Just as babies need calming routines, so do mothers. A quiet cup of tea, dim lights,

soft music — these habits are not indulgent. They're grounding.

6. Realistic Expectations

You are not meant to do this perfectly. Not every bedtime will go to plan. Not every night will be restful. Resilience grows not from control, but from flexibility and kindness.

In the world of infant sleep support, it's easy to focus entirely on the child. But you are not a machine. You are a human — with a nervous system, with needs, with feelings — who deserves sleep too.

Your child's wellbeing matters. But so does yours.

As we move into the next chapter and begin exploring the **attachment bond**, I invite you to carry this with you: Sleep support isn't about pushing your child into change. It's about **creating conditions that support everyone's nervous system — including yours — to feel safer, calmer, and more connected**.

Parent Reflection:

What feels hardest about sleep in this season of parenting?

How is it affecting me — emotionally, physically, relationally?

Have I absorbed any messages (from family, social media, books) that make me feel like I'm doing it "wrong"?

How have those voices shaped my expectations of myself?

What does sleep loss cost me — beyond just tiredness?

How does it influence my thoughts, identity, or ability to cope?

What do I feel guilty about, and what would I say to a friend who felt the same?

Could I offer myself even a fraction of that compassion?

If I could give myself one permission slip right now, what would it be?

Permission to rest? To ask for help? To not get it perfect?

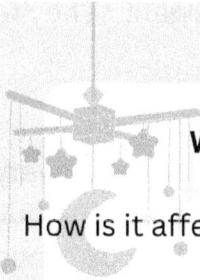

Chapter 3

Sleep and the Attachment Bond
What Attachment Really Means — and Why It's Not Fragile

One of the most common fears parents bring into conversations about sleep is this:

> *"If I help my child sleep differently, will it damage our bond?"*

It's a powerful question — and it comes from a good place. Our bond with our child is sacred. When that bond feels at risk, whether from exhaustion, separation, or a new routine, it can stir up a tidal wave of doubt.

But here's what I want you to hear — clearly, confidently, and with the weight of both research and real-world experience behind it:

You can change your child's sleep habits **without breaking their trust**.

You can set boundaries around sleep **without threatening attachment**.

And most importantly, **attachment is not that fragile**.

In this chapter, we'll explore what attachment actually is, how it develops, and why secure attachment can coexist — beautifully — with gentle, structured sleep support.

What Is Attachment, Really?

Attachment is not about being attached at all times. It's not about co-sleeping, babywearing, or responding instantly to every cry — although those things can all be part of a healthy bond.

Attachment is about a **child's internal sense of safety**. It's the belief they develop, over time, that says:

- I matter

- Someone will come when I need them

- I am safe in the world

- My feelings are important

- I can handle hard things because someone will help me

The foundations of attachment are laid through consistent, emotionally attuned caregiving. That doesn't mean perfection — it means **good enough**. And it happens through hundreds of small interactions over months and years.

The Four Pillars of Secure Attachment

Decades of research in developmental psychology tell us that secure attachment is shaped by four key behaviours from caregivers:

1. Consistency
Children feel secure when responses are generally predictable. That doesn't mean always getting it right, but rather being emotionally available more often than not.

2. Sensitivity

Caregivers notice cues, interpret them accurately, and respond in ways that meet the child's needs. Sensitivity is not just about speed — it's about *attunement*.

3. Emotional Availability

The caregiver can handle the child's big feelings without becoming overwhelmed, dismissive, or punishing.

4. Repair

When things go wrong — because they will — the caregiver returns, reconnects, and repairs the rupture. This teaches the child that relationships are resilient.

What's not included in this model? Never letting your child cry. Being physically present 24/7. Always saying yes. These ideas are common in modern parenting rhetoric, but they're not what secure attachment requires.

Crying Isn't Always a Threat to Attachment

Let's tackle one of the biggest myths directly:

"If a baby cries during sleep support, they'll feel abandoned and lose trust in me."

This fear is understandable — crying hits us at a biological level. But it's not always a sign of harm.

In a safe, connected, responsive relationship, **crying can also be a form of communication, protest, or adjustment**. When a child experiences a new routine or a shift in support, it's natural for them to express frustration. That doesn't mean they feel unsafe — it means they're expressing themselves in the only way they can.

Here's the difference:

- Crying **with** a responsive caregiver nearby = protest, signalling, processing.

- Crying **without** support or repair = risk of dysregulation, insecurity, or distress.

What matters is the *context* of the crying:

- Is the caregiver emotionally present, even if not holding or feeding?

- Is the child's nervous system supported with rhythm, predictability, and care?

- Is there repair and reconnection after periods of upset?

If the answer is yes, attachment is not harmed — it's being *strengthened* through trust and containment.

Can Boundaries Strengthen Attachment?

Absolutely. In fact, **boundaries are a key component of secure attachment**.

Children feel safe when they know their caregivers are in charge — not in a harsh or authoritarian way, but in a calm, confident, reliable way.

Sleep support often involves boundary setting:

- "This is bedtime now."

- "I'll stay with you, but I won't pick you up again tonight."

- "We're done with the third cup of water."

These limits are not cold. They're **clear**. And they provide structure within which the child can rest.

When boundaries are combined with warmth, attunement, and repair, they become **protective** — not damaging.

Co-Sleeping, Sleep Training, and Attachment: Clearing Up the Confusion

One of the reasons parents feel so unsure about sleep decisions is that sleep practices often get *mistaken* for attachment measures.

Practice	Attachment Status
Co-sleeping	Can support secure attachment — if parent is attuned and child is comforted. Not required.
Separate sleep space	Also can support secure attachment — especially if bedtime routines are warm and consistent.
Sleep training	Can be attachment-safe when done gradually, with attunement and repair.
No sleep training	Also fine — as long as the parent can sustain the routine without resentment or depletion.

In other words, **attachment is built in your daytime relationship, not determined by your bedtime method**.

What matters more than where your child sleeps is *how emotionally held they feel in the relationship overall*.

When Parents Feel Torn

It's not uncommon to feel deeply conflicted:

- You *want* to be responsive, but you're *burning out*

- You *believe* in co-sleeping, but no one is sleeping well

- You *tried* sleep training, but it felt wrong for your child

- You're *desperate* for a solution, but afraid of doing damage

Let's name that for what it is: the tension between love and limits, instinct and exhaustion.

And let's offer this framing instead:

> You're not choosing between connection and
> rest.
> You're choosing to support both — in a way
> that evolves as your child grows.

This is where **attachment-informed behavioural support** lives. Not in rigid rules or extreme positions, but in the thoughtful middle ground — where structure and sensitivity work together.

In the next chapter, we'll introduce one of the most important ideas in this book: **emotional safety in sleep work**.

We'll explore:

- How your child's nervous system responds to change

- Why "just let them cry" often misses the point

- How to build a plan that reduces stress, not adds to it — for everyone involved

Because the goal isn't just for your child to sleep. It's for your family to feel more rested, more connected, and more confident in the path you're choosing.

Parent Reflection:

How do I define a "secure attachment" in my own parenting mind?
Where did that definition come from? Books, social media, my upbringing?

Do I ever feel torn between being responsive and needing rest or structure?
When do those feelings come up the most?

What does my child already show me about feeling safe with me?
Are there little signs — a look, a cuddle, a reach for my hand — that tell me our bond is strong, even when things aren't perfect?

What fears do I hold about making changes to sleep?
What do I worry it might say about me as a parent?

What would it feel like to trust that structure and attachment can co-exist?

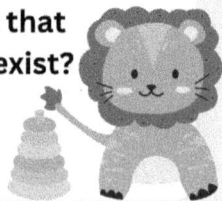

Chapter 4

Emotional Safety in Sleep Work
Why How We Do It Matters Just as Much as What We Do

Let's begin with a foundational truth: Every sleep intervention has an emotional footprint.

Not because sleep training is inherently damaging — but because how we introduce change, how we respond to stress, and how the child experiences the transition deeply shapes their ability to adapt and feel safe.

This chapter is your compass. It offers a way to navigate sleep support through the lens of emotional safety — so that whatever plan you implement, it is grounded in trust, relationship, and regulation.

Because attachment-informed doesn't mean never setting boundaries. It means we consider:

- The child's nervous system

- The parent's wellbeing

- The emotional *experience* of any strategy, not just the behavioural goal

Let's explore what emotional safety looks like, why it matters, and how to embed it into every step of sleep support. Emotional safety is the internal sense that says:

- *I am safe here*

- *My needs will be understood*

- *My emotions won't overwhelm or threaten the person I rely on*

- *Even when things are hard, I won't be left alone in my distress*

For babies and young children, emotional safety doesn't come from explanations or logic — it comes from nervous system cues. Children feel emotionally safe when:

- Our tone of voice is calm

- Our body is regulated (not rushed, harsh, or frustrated)

- Our responses are predictable

- There is a balance of comfort and containment

We can't *protect* children from all frustration. But we can help them tolerate it — and that's where emotional safety makes all the difference.

Stress Isn't Always a Problem — But Dysregulation Is

One of the common misconceptions around attachment and sleep support is that all stress is harmful.

Not true.

Babies and toddlers *can* experience stress and still feel safe — provided that stress is manageable, time-limited, and supported. In fact, learning to move through tolerable stress with the help of a caregiver is what builds resilience.

What becomes harmful is:

- Prolonged, unrelieved stress

- Unattuned responses from caregivers

- The absence of repair when things go wrong

Let's return to Polyvagal Theory, as introduced in Chapter 1. According to Dr Stephen Porges, the nervous system is always scanning for cues of safety or danger. When a child's cues of distress go unanswered for too long — especially in the early months — their nervous system may shift from protest (sympathetic activation) into shut-down (dorsal vagal collapse). This is not regulation — it's disconnection.

That's why emotional safety is *not* about removing all struggle. It's about providing enough co-regulation that the child can tolerate the stress of change — and still feel emotionally connected to their caregiver.

A Regulated Parent Is the Child's Greatest Sleep Tool

Children co-regulate with our nervous systems long before they internalise self-soothing tools of their own. In other words: Your calm is their anchor.   Your breath, posture, voice, and presence all shape their ability to rest.

This doesn't mean you must be zen at all times (we're human, not robots). But it does mean that prioritising your own regulation is not selfish — it's strategic. Sleep support becomes more effective — and less emotionally loaded — when the adult is:

- Calm enough to follow through

- Grounded enough to soothe or contain emotion

- Aware of their own triggers (like the sound of crying)

- Able to stay emotionally present, even when setting limits

Before implementing any sleep change, it's worth asking:

> *How regulated do I feel right now?*
> *What's my nervous system doing when bedtime begins?*
> *Am I trying to fix sleep from a place of panic or pressure, or from a place of compassion and readiness?*

Sleep Work That Prioritises Emotional Safety Looks Like...

Here are some of the key features of emotionally safe sleep support:

Preparation

- You introduce change gradually, with clear cues

- You talk to older babies/toddlers using simple, reassuring language

- You make environmental changes (room, cot, light, routine) gently and predictably

Presence

- You remain physically or emotionally available during harder moments

- If crying occurs, it's heard and witnessed — not dismissed or ignored

- You offer calming cues like voice, hand, or eye contact, depending on what soothes your child

Flexibility

- You watch for signs of overwhelm and adjust accordingly

- You consider temperament and adapt methods as needed

- You allow pauses or breaks if someone is too dysregulated to continue

Repair

- You reconnect after stressful moments (e.g. cuddles, kind words, snuggling the next morning)

- You narrate the experience in age-appropriate language ("You were upset last night, but Mummy was there. You're safe, and we're learning together.")

What Emotional Safety Is *Not*

It's also important to understand that emotional safety:

- Is not the same as avoiding all tears

- Is not the same as always saying yes

- Is not the same as doing nothing and hoping sleep improves on its own

Tears can be part of change. Boundaries can exist without coldness. And you can support your child through frustration without rescuing them from every moment of discomfort. Emotionally safe sleep support means:

I'm here. I see you. I won't abandon you.
And I also believe you're capable of learning
new ways to rest.

That balance — between containment and compassion — is the heart of this book.

You Matter Too

In this chapter, we've focused a lot on the child's nervous system. But emotional safety applies to *you*, too. You deserve to feel safe in the process. You deserve to know that your instincts will be honoured, not overridden. You deserve a plan that fits *your* family, not just a textbook.

In the next chapter, we'll begin building that plan. We'll explore the Ladder of Sleep Support — a layered, flexible approach that starts with emotional foundations and gradually introduces behavioural strategies that respect the attachment bond.

Because the best sleep plans don't just work.
They work *with* you — not against you.

When I first met *Alyssa*, she was a mum of two — a bright three-year-old and a ten-month-old baby named Max. She came to our session looking completely depleted. "I just don't know what else to try," she said. "Everyone keeps telling me I need to be tougher — that I'm spoiling Max. But I can't just leave him to cry like that."

Alyssa had already attempted a few sleep training methods. One friend swore by controlled crying; another recommended she "just stop going in altogether." Every time she tried to ignore Max's cries, she ended up sobbing outside the door herself. "I feel like I'm failing twice," she said. "I'm either ruining his sleep, or I'm ruining his trust in me."

When we explored Max's sleep patterns, it was clear he had strong sleep associations: he needed to be rocked or held every time he woke, and bedtime took up to two hours each night. Alyssa's exhaustion was real — but so was her deep instinct to stay emotionally present for her baby.

Rather than focusing on stopping the crying, we took a different approach: supporting Max's emotions while gently teaching him new sleep skills.

We talked about emotional safety, and how it wasn't about preventing all discomfort — but rather about staying with our children through it. We reframed crying as a form of communication, not manipulation. Alyssa said she felt instant relief just knowing she didn't have to choose between supporting Max emotionally and improving his sleep.

We created a plan that included verbal reassurance, consistent touch, and gradually decreasing Alyssa's physical involvement at bedtime. At first, she sat beside the cot, hand on Max's back, singing quietly. Then, over the following weeks, she shifted to sitting nearby, then outside the door with the door open. She always responded to his cries, but in ways that gently nudged him toward settling in new ways.

Alyssa started journaling how she felt each night, which gave her space to reflect on Max's progress and her own confidence. "He still cries sometimes," she told me by Week 3. "But now it sounds different. It's like he's saying, 'Okay, this is hard, but I know you're there.' And I think I needed that too."

By Week 5, Max was falling asleep within 15 minutes most nights. Alyssa described feeling calmer — more in sync with herself as a mother. She wasn't ignoring Max's needs anymore; she was meeting them in a new way.

This is what emotionally safe sleep work looks like. It doesn't mean no tears, no limits, or no change. It means guiding children with presence, patience, and attunement — even when the road is bumpy.

Parent Reflection:

Use this space to check in with yourself — not as a "sleep manager," but as a caregiver with feelings, instincts, and needs of your own.

When my child struggles to sleep, what happens in my body?

Do I feel tense, agitated, helpless, calm? Do I notice any patterns in how I respond?

What messages have I absorbed about crying, frustration, or limits?

Am I trying to avoid all protest — or feeling pressured to push through discomfort?

What helps me feel emotionally safe at bedtime?

Is it having a plan, being with a partner, lowering the lights, turning off my phone, or something else?

What kind of emotional cues am I giving at bedtime?

How might my child be reading my tone, pace, or energy?

If I could give my child one unspoken message about bedtime, what would it be?

Could it sound something like: "You're safe. You can rest. I'm here, and we're learning together."

Chapter 5

The Ladder of Sleep Support

A Step-by-Step Framework That Protects Connection While Building Better Sleep

Now, we've laid the emotional foundation for what healthy, attachment-informed sleep support looks like. You understand the difference between self-soothing and self-settling. You've explored how boundaries and connection can coexist. And you've reflected on your own role as a regulated presence in the bedtime experience.

So the next question is:

Where do I actually begin?

That's where the Ladder of Sleep Support comes in.

This isn't a one-size-fits-all solution or a rigid checklist. It's a flexible framework — designed to meet you and your child exactly where you're at, and offer the next gentle step forward.

Why a Ladder?

Imagine sleep support as a ladder with four main rungs. Each rung builds on the one below, offering a sturdy foundation before introducing something new.

You can climb gradually — at your own pace — and pause or move back down if needed.

This approach is about:

- Honouring your child's emotional and developmental readiness

- Respecting your parenting values

- Matching the level of support to the level of need

Some families may only need the first few steps. Others may move all the way up to more structured behavioural interventions — but with *emotional safety* at every rung.

The Four Rungs of the Ladder of Sleep Support

Here's a visual summary of the model, which we'll explore in more depth below:

Ladder of Sleep Support

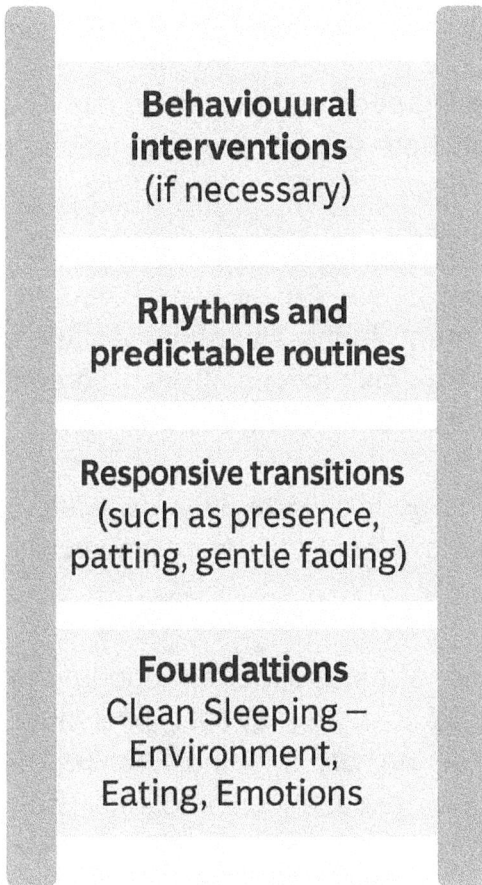

Behaviouural interventions
(if necessary)

Rhythms and predictable routines

Responsive transitions
(such as presence, patting, gentle fading)

Foundattions
Clean Sleeping –
Environment,
Eating, Emotions

Let's walk through each rung.

Rung 1: Foundations

Clean Sleeping — Environment, Eating, Emotions

Before addressing bedtime resistance, night wakings, or habits, we start here — with the foundations that allow sleep to *occur at all*.

This includes:

- Environment: Is the sleep space dark, quiet, and safe? Are distractions (toys, screens, noise) reduced?

- Eating: Is your child hungry, over-full, or feeding too close to sleep? Are there issues with reflux or digestion?

- Emotions: What happened during the day? Is your child carrying stress, overstimulation, or separation anxiety into the evening? How does your child experience emotional co-regulation throughout the day?

When these elements are out of balance, no amount of sleep training will stick. Children need to feel *safe*, *fed*, and *settled* before they can drift off — even with help.

This step also includes checking in with your own foundation: Are you regulated enough to support bedtime calmly? Are you well-resourced to begin sleep changes?

Rung 2: Rhythms and Predictable Routines

Helping the Body Clock Feel Safe

Sleep is rhythmic. Our bodies thrive on predictability — and so do our children.

Here we focus on:

- Daily sleep timing: Is your child's nap schedule age-appropriate? Are they overtired or under-tired at bedtime?

- Bedtime routine: Are the steps of your bedtime predictable and calming — for both child and parent?

- Consistency across caregivers: Are routines similar across the week or with different adults?

This stage is not about strictness. It's about rhythm — the cues and signals that help the body and brain anticipate sleep. When the rhythm is steady, your child's nervous system can begin to let go of hypervigilance and move toward rest.

Rung 3: Responsive Transitions

Staying Present While Reducing Sleep Associations

This rung is where many gentle families do the bulk of their sleep work.

Here, we start to help the child shift from needing sleep *done to them* (rocking, feeding to sleep) toward falling asleep *with us nearby but doing less*.

This might involve:

- Sitting next to the cot or bed, with your hand on them

- Using rhythmic voice or touch, but gradually reducing it

- Introducing a transitional object (like a lovey or blanket)

- Using "fading" techniques to slowly reduce support over days or weeks

These transitions are still emotionally rich — the child is not left alone. But they begin to experience the possibility of falling asleep with *less* help, without feeling abandoned.

This is a particularly powerful rung for anxious children, parents recovering from difficult postpartum periods, or families who want to keep the bond close while still inviting more independence.

Rung 4: Behavioural Interventions

Introducing Structure Without Sacrificing Safety

This is the top rung of the ladder — not because it's better, but because it relies on the stability of what's come before.

Here, we're introducing more structured behavioural approaches, such as:

- Fading: Gradually reducing parental presence at bedtime, or Camping Out: Staying in the room, slowly increasing distance

- Graduated Extinction or Responsive Settling (Controlled Crying): Increasing time between check-ins, while monitoring for regulation

- Monitored Settling: our method that builds on responsive settling but removes rigid rules

- Bedtime Passes, Sticker Charts, Sleep Rules: Especially for older children who benefit from visual structure or incentives

These interventions *can* be used in emotionally safe ways — when:

- They're implemented gently

- The child's nervous system is ready

- There's repair, warmth, and predictability

- The parent is regulated and supported

Behavioural interventions without relationship are simply enforcement. But behavioural interventions *with* connection become powerful tools of learning and growth.

Choosing Your Step

Here's the beauty of the ladder:

- You can start wherever your child needs support

- You can stay on a rung for days, weeks, or longer

- You can pause, move back down, or mix approaches as needed

If you're not sure where to begin, start by strengthening the foundations. Even small changes to bedtime routine or sleep environment can unlock improvements — no tears required.

In the chapters that follow, we'll explore each rung of the ladder in greater detail — starting with Clean Sleeping Foundations in Chapter 6.

You'll learn how to:

- Create a sleep-conducive environment

- Tweak feeding, lighting, and emotional cues

- Understand common pitfalls that sabotage rest

- Identify what's working — and what's not

This is where theory begins to meet practice — and where real change begins.

Because better sleep isn't just a destination. It's a process of gentle, supported shifts — step by step, rung by rung.

And you're climbing it together.

Chapter 6

Clean Sleeping Foundations

Setting the Stage for Rest with Environment, Eating, and Emotions

Sleep is not something we force. It's something we support. Before we consider structured routines or behavioural strategies, we first need to ask:

> *Is the body ready for sleep?*
> *Is the space inviting rest?*
> *Is the nervous system calm enough to let go?*

In many cases, persistent sleep challenges aren't the result of faulty parenting or a "bad sleeper." They're rooted in overlooked foundations — subtle factors that, when addressed, can make a world of difference.

This chapter introduces those foundational elements —
what I call Clean Sleeping:

- A restful environment

- Appropriate nutrition and timing

- Awareness of emotional regulation — both for the
  child and caregiver

These may seem simple at first glance. But together,
they create the conditions in which your sleep plan can
take root — gently and effectively.

Environment: The Unsung Hero of Sleep Support

Our environment tells our nervous system what to
expect. Just as the smell of popcorn might make you
crave a movie night, the right cues in a child's room help
their body and brain prepare for rest.

Here's what to consider:

Darkness.

Melatonin — the body's natural sleepy hormone — is suppressed by light, especially blue light.

- Use blackout blinds or temporary darkening solutions (even taped-up cardboard can work!)

- Dim lights for 30–60 minutes before bedtime

- Avoid bright overhead lighting and screens in the hour leading up to sleep

Temperature.

As mentioned in earlier chapters, cooler environments support melatonin release and deeper sleep.

- Ideal sleep temperature: 18–21°C (64–70°F)

- Dress your child in breathable, natural fibres

- Avoid overheating — one more layer than you're wearing is often enough

Noise.
Sudden changes in sound are more disruptive than consistent low-level noise.

- Use white noise to mask environmental sounds

- Choose a sound machine with a low, steady hum (avoid lullabies or ocean waves, which may vary too much)

- Avoid placing the machine right next to your child's head

Visual Clutter.
Overstimulating rooms can keep children mentally alert, even when tired.

- Simplify the sleep space — tidy toys, calm colours, fewer distractions

- Avoid light-up mobiles or projectors once the child is past infancy

- Keep books or comfort objects accessible, but limited

Associations and Location.
Is the bed associated with rest — or play, conflict, stress?

- Avoid using the cot or bed for time-outs

- Keep the room a peaceful zone, not one where discipline or chaos regularly happens

- If you're transitioning to a new sleep space, spend calm daytime moments in there first to build comfort

Eating: Fuel for Sleep — or a Hindrance?

Nutrition and timing play a powerful, often underestimated role in sleep.

Key considerations:

Timing of Last Meal or Milk Feed

- Infants may need a full feed before sleep to sustain longer stretches

- Older toddlers and preschoolers may sleep more soundly if dinner isn't too close to bedtime (aim for 60–90 minutes before)

- Light bedtime snacks can help if dinner is early — think banana, wholegrain toast, or warm milk

Sugar and Artificial Additives

- Excess sugar or food colouring close to bed can overstimulate

- Watch for hidden sugars in cereals, yoghurts, and "treats" given close to bedtime

Sleep Associations
For babies and toddlers:

- Feeding to sleep is common and not always problematic — but if it's the *only* way your child falls asleep, and you're experiencing night waking challenges, it may be something to gradually shift

Reflux, Wind, or Discomfort

- Are they wriggling, arching, unsettled shortly after feeding?

- Is there a known or suspected food intolerance or allergy?

- Consult with your GP, child health nurse, or paediatric dietitian if feeding-related discomfort is impacting rest

Emotions: The Invisible Weight on Sleep

Even when the body is fed and the room is dark, sleep can still be elusive — because of what's happening inside your child's emotional world.

Children process the day through their bodies. If something stressful, exciting, confusing or overwhelming has happened, it often surfaces at bedtime.

Signs that emotional tension is interfering with sleep:

- Your child seems *wired* even when tired (a cortisol spike)

- They suddenly cling, resist, or avoid bedtime

- They want "one more" of everything — stories, drinks, cuddles, reassurance

- They show big feelings just before bed (crying, tantrums, fear)

What helps:

1. Gentle Wind-Down Routines

- Keep the last hour of the day low-stimulation

- Predictable routines act as emotional anchors ("First bath, then books, then sleep")

- Use soft voices, gentle touch, and fewer decisions ("It's time for bed" instead of "Do you want to go to bed?")

2. Connection Time
Children crave reconnection after separation or stimulation.

- Five minutes of one-on-one play (even silly or light-hearted) before bedtime can reduce clingy behaviour

- For older children, offer space to "unpack" their day before bed

3. Co-Regulation Tools

- Breathing together

- Guided imagery ("Let's float on a cloud together")

- Gentle massage or calming scents (lavender, if your child enjoys it)

- Validating language: "You're safe. I'll help you rest."

4. Your Own State

- If you're stressed, anxious or rushing, your child *will* pick it up

- Take 30 seconds to centre yourself before starting bedtime — deep breath, stretch, short pause

- Let bedtime become a shared *exhale*, not a power struggle

These foundations — environment, eating, and emotions — don't always get the spotlight. But they are the soil in which every other sleep strategy is planted.

When these three areas are calm, consistent, and regulated, sleep becomes *easier*. Sometimes, sleep improves significantly with no additional changes.

This is especially true for sensitive children, neurodivergent children, or those recovering from disrupted sleep patterns — illness, transitions, separation, or trauma.

If things feel stuck, come back to this chapter. Ask yourself: Have I looked at all three foundation zones clearly? Have I been expecting change without first creating the conditions for change?

In Chapter 7, we'll move up to the next rung of the Ladder: Rhythms and Predictable Routines.

We'll explore:

- Age-appropriate nap patterns

- The myth of "bedtime resistance"

- How to support the body clock

- Realistic routines that work for *your* family

Because even gentle plans need rhythm — and rhythm brings safety.

Parent Reflection:

Take a few moments to reflect on the everyday conditions that set the stage for sleep in your home. This is not about perfection — it's about awareness and curiosity.

What is the atmosphere like in our child's sleep space?

Is it dark, quiet, calming — or do we notice stimulation, clutter, or disruption?

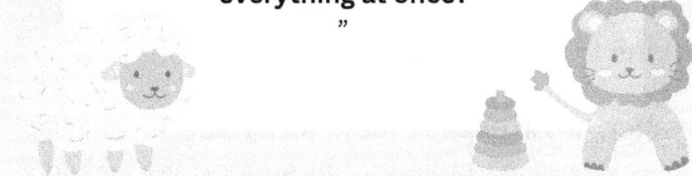

What does our evening rhythm feel like?

Are there regular steps and calming cues, or are we rushing or improvising night to night?

How does feeding impact our sleep routine?

Are there patterns of feeding-to-sleep that feel helpful... or unhelpful?

How might emotions (mine or my child's) be carried into bedtime?

What can I do to create a sense of unwinding, connection, or calm?

What small, simple shift could I make this week that might support rest — without needing to "fix" everything at once?

"

Chapter 7

Rhythms and Predictable Routines
Helping Your Child's Body Clock Feel Safe

If you've ever been told, *"You just need a better routine"*, and felt like screaming — you're not alone.

The advice often feels dismissive, like all your exhaustion could be fixed if you'd just stick to a more rigid schedule. But here's what I want you to know: Routines are not about control. They're about rhythm — and rhythm helps everyone, especially children, feel safe.

Just as your child's nervous system responds to emotional consistency, it also thrives on temporal consistency — patterns in when we eat, play, rest, and sleep. When these rhythms are predictable (not perfect), the body starts to anticipate what's coming next.

In this chapter, we'll explore how to establish realistic, emotionally supportive routines that support your child's natural sleep biology — without becoming rigid, exhausting, or incompatible with your family life.

What We Mean by "Rhythm"

Sleep rhythms are internal cycles governed by your child's circadian rhythm and sleep pressure systems.

Let's define those simply:

Circadian Rhythm - The body's internal 24-hour clock that regulates sleep and wake cycles, guided by exposure to light and darkness.

Sleep Pressure (Homeostatic Drive) - This builds while your child is awake. The longer they're up, the stronger the need to sleep becomes — until they get overtired, which can spike cortisol and make falling asleep harder.

These systems work together. And when they're supported with consistent routines and well-timed naps or bedtimes, your child is more likely to:

- Fall asleep more easily

- Sleep longer and more deeply

- Wake more predictably

- Feel calmer and more emotionally regulated during the day

Understanding Circadian Rhythms: Why Babies Don't Sleep Like Adults (Yet)

If you've ever wondered *why* your newborn wakes at night like it's party time, or why your six-month-old suddenly starts waking at 5:00 a.m. — the answer might lie in their **circadian rhythm**.

Our **circadian rhythm** is like the body's internal clock. It governs the 24-hour sleep–wake cycle, regulating when we feel alert, when we get drowsy, and when our body starts winding down for rest. It's primarily influenced by **light and darkness**, though other biological processes like **body temperature, digestion, and hormone release** also play a role.

So When Does a Baby's Circadian Rhythm Actually Start?

Not right away.

A newborn arrives without a mature circadian rhythm — that means their internal system hasn't yet learned to tell day from night. Sleep in the early months is patchy, irregular, and driven more by **hunger, digestion, and comfort** than by body clock patterns.

You can think of the newborn phase as running on *survival mode* — sleeping around the clock in scattered bursts, not because they're misbehaving, but because their biological systems are still booting up.

- Around **6 weeks**, circadian rhythms begin to **emerge**, as melatonin and cortisol production start to follow a more daily rhythm.

- By **3–6 months**, most babies have developed a more regular sleep–wake pattern — although not necessarily sleeping through the night.

- This age range (4–6 months) is often when sleep issues first emerge, precisely *because* the circadian rhythm is becoming more defined.

Many families report that "everything was fine — until it wasn't." That turning point often coincides with a developmental leap in sleep biology.

The Science of Sleep Stages

As part of understanding infant sleep rhythms, it's helpful to know that babies — like adults — move through **sleep cycles** made up of two main phases:

1. **Non-REM (Quiet) Sleep**:

     o   Deep, restorative sleep

     o   Blood flow to muscles increases

     o   Tissue repair and growth hormone release occur

- The body is very still — this is the *"hard to wake"* phase

2. **REM (Active) Sleep**:

   - Brain is active, dreams occur

   - Breathing and heart rate are irregular

   - Babies may twitch, suck, or move around

   - The body is "on" internally, even if it looks restful

In early infancy, babies spend about **50% of their sleep in each state**, and sleep cycles are **short** — just **40 to 50 minutes**. By preschool age, children move toward **90-minute sleep cycles**, like adults.

Sleep Builds Brains

Sleep is always important — but for babies, it's absolutely foundational. While adults use sleep to restore energy, consolidate memories, and repair cells, **infants are actively building their brains during sleep**.

When we say sleep is essential for development, we're not exaggerating:

- Synapses form and strengthen during sleep

- Memory pathways consolidate

- Emotional regulation circuits develop

- Growth hormone is released

In short, babies don't just *rest* during sleep — they *develop*.

Circadian Rhythms and Body Temperature

One of the lesser-known drivers of our circadian rhythm is **body temperature**.

- Around **10 p.m.**, body temperature is usually at its **highest**

- Between **4:00 and 5:00 a.m.**, it reaches its **lowest point**

This natural drop in temperature is one reason **early rising** is so common in babies and toddlers. Combine a cool room with a cool body — and you have a recipe for pre-dawn wake-ups. Add a light sleeper or a child who's already fragmented in their sleep, and it's no surprise they pop up at 4:45 a.m. wide-eyed and ready for the day.

We'll look at how to support these early risers more in the chapter on common sleep scenarios, but just know — this is a *normal biological occurrence*, and not necessarily a sign of poor parenting or bad habits.

What About Feeding at Night?

It's worth noting that, biologically, most healthy babies **can sleep through the night** (without needing feeds) by about **6–9 months**. However, that doesn't mean they *all* *do.* And it certainly doesn't mean they *should*, or that you're doing something wrong if yours doesn't.

In fact, many sleep professionals — myself included — question the overly optimistic statistics that say "80% of babies sleep through the night by nine months." If that were true, most of us in the sleep world would be out of a job.

In reality:

- Every baby is different

- Some babies are developmentally ready, but still reliant on habits

- Others have unmet needs (nutrition, comfort, routine) that need gentle support

- And some simply haven't made the shift yet — but will, with time and guidance

Newborn Sleep at a Glance

Newborns (0–3 months) sleep:

- In multiple short chunks

- Day and night, without a clear pattern

- Anywhere from **10.5 to 18 hours** in 24 hours

- With wake windows that vary from 30 minutes to 3 hours

Their sleep is heavily influenced by:

- Feeding needs

- Digestion

- Comfort and regulation

They may sleep 15 minutes… or 3 hours. Their twitching, sucking, or wriggling in sleep is normal. So is needing contact or motion to settle.

If it feels chaotic — it's not you. It's biology.

So What Helps?

The most powerful way to support circadian development is to align with your child's natural rhythms:

- Expose them to **natural light** during the day (especially morning)

- Keep lights low and consistent in the evening

- Offer a **gentle, predictable bedtime routine**

- Keep the sleep environment **dark, cool, and quiet**

- Avoid overstimulation in the hour before bed

- Focus on **regulation** before independence

The Power of Predictable Routines

Predictability doesn't mean a military schedule. It means your child's body and brain are learning: *"This comes next. I'm safe."* Routines do more than manage logistics — they become a form of **emotional safety**. When a child knows what to expect:

- Anxiety lowers

- Power struggles reduce

- Sleep transitions become easier

Even babies start to anticipate bedtime when there are repeated cues — like dim lights, soft music, or the same series of calming steps each night.

The best routines are:

1. Simple
No long to-do list. A few consistent steps are all you need — e.g., bath, books, cuddles, lights out.

2. Sustainable
Can you follow it even on difficult nights? When your partner's not home? When you're tired?

3. Soothing
Is the pace slow enough to downshift? Or are you rushing, bargaining, or negotiating every step?

4. Sensory-Smart

Children are sensory beings. Calming routines often use:

- Dim lighting

- Warm bath or massage

- Gentle music or white noise

- Consistent bedtime story voice

- Soft textures (blanket, teddy, pyjamas)

5. Social

Connection is the goal. It's not about making bedtime a performance — it's about relational cues that help your child feel safe to let go.

Timing Matters

Let's talk about **biological sleep windows**. These are periods when your child is naturally more primed to fall asleep. Miss the window, and they may get overtired (hello, second wind). Catch it, and sleep often comes more smoothly. While every child is unique, here are rough bedtime and nap patterns by age. The following tables outline typical nap schedules and bedtimes by age group. These reflect general averages; some children may vary up to 30–60 minutes in either direction. This schedule is based on professional experience as providing for optimal success, however, I take no offence if you disagree and would like to try your own schedule.

Newborns

Age	Total Sleep	Wake Window	Naps per Day	Bedtime Range
0–6 weeks	14–18 hrs	45–60 mins	4	Varies; often 9–11pm
6–12 weeks	14–17 hrs	60–90 mins	4	Shifting earlier: 8–10pm

Infants

Age	Wake Windows	Nap	Ideal Bedtime Range
3–4 months	75–120 mins	3-4	7:30–9:00pm
5–6 months	2–2.5 hrs	3	6:30–8:00pm
7–8 months	2.5–3 hrs	2–3 *	6:00–7:30pm
9–12 months	3–4 hrs	2	6:00–7:30pm

*aim to drop the third nap at 7 months, with a micro nap at the end of the day in case of 'emergency' only... to avoid interruptions during the night sleep.

Toddlers

Age	Nap Schedule	Bedtime Range
12–18 months	1–2 naps (transitioning to 1)*	6:30–7:30pm
18–24 months	1 nap (1–2 hrs around midday)	6:30–7:30pm
2–3 years	1 nap (may shorten or resist)	6:30–8:00pm

*aim to drop the second nap at 13 months, with a micro nap at the end of the day in case of 'emergency' only... to avoid interruptions during the night sleep.

Pre-Schooler

Age	Nap Schedule	Bedtime Range
3–4 years	Nap is phased out with quiet rest time	6:30–7:30pm
4–5 years	No nap	6:30–8:00pm

These aren't rules. They're rhythms — and they're meant to be flexible. Children with neurodevelopmental differences (like autism or ADHD) may have different timing needs altogether.

What matters most is that you notice your own child's patterns:

- When do they seem naturally tired?

- When are they most alert and active?

- Do they wake at a consistent time regardless of bedtime?

These clues can help you adjust sleep timing to better align with *their* biology, not the one in a book.

Parent Reflection:

Take a moment to pause and gently reflect on the natural patterns — or chaos! — in your current sleep rhythm. This isn't about blame. It's about tuning into what's already there and what might help next.

What parts of our day already feel rhythmic or predictable?
Do we tend to follow a loose pattern with meals, naps, or bedtime steps — even unintentionally?

What part of the day feels most rushed, stressful, or inconsistent?
Is it mornings, dinnertime, the bedtime wind-down, or overnight wake-ups?

What is one small routine that my child seems to anticipate or enjoy?
It could be a bedtime song, favourite book, or how we turn off the light. These cues matter more than we realise.

Is our current routine sustainable for me?
Can I keep this up on hard nights, with both kids, or when I'm alone?

If I could add or change just one thing to support our rhythm this week — what would I try?

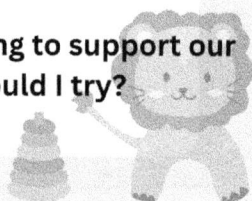

Troubleshooting the Routine Struggles

Even predictable routines can run into trouble. Let's look at a few common roadblocks.

Bedtime Resistance

Often a sign of:

- Over or under tiredness

- Inconsistent routine

- Power struggles during the wind-down

- Fear, anxiety, or wanting more connection

Try this:

- Offer 10 minutes of 1:1 "child-led" play before beginning the bedtime routine

- Use visual schedules or bedtime cards for toddlers

- Narrate the routine with gentle authority: *"Now it's story time. Next is lights out."*

Nap Refusal

Often a sign of:

- Nap timing being too early or too late

- The child beginning to transition nap stages

- Needing a calmer pre-nap wind down (yes, even for naps)

Second Wind

When children miss their natural sleep window, cortisol kicks in — and they suddenly seem "wired."

- Aim for earlier, not later, bedtime if you're unsure

- Begin wind-down **before** overtired signs appear

Some families feel nervous about routine because it feels rigid. But rhythm is not rigidity. It's a supportive structure that allows for adaptation.

For example:

- On holiday? Keep the steps, adjust the timing.

- Rough day? Drop the bath, keep the books and cuddle.

- Child sick? Stay flexible, but keep wind-down cues in place.

The body remembers what the brain can't organise. Even when life gets messy, maintaining some rhythm helps the nervous system feel held.

This isn't about crafting the "perfect" schedule. It's about knowing that sleep is biological, but also relational. Routine is physical, but also emotional. Predictability supports not just sleep — but trust. When we offer rhythm, we're not just managing the clock. We're saying to our child:

"You can rest now. You're safe. We know what to expect — together."

When I first met Ava, she was beyond exhausted. Her little boy, Liam, was 11 months old and waking frequently during the night — sometimes five or six times — with no discernible pattern. Ava described their days as "chaotic but well-intentioned." Meals, naps, and bedtime all happened eventually, but there was no consistent rhythm from one day to the next. Ava was trying to respond to Liam's cues, but as she admitted, "He just seems tired all the time… and so am I."

We began by mapping out Liam's current sleep, feeding, and activity patterns. What stood out immediately was that everything shifted depending on how the night had gone. If Liam had a rough night, Ava would let him sleep in. Naps would happen at varying times and lengths, sometimes in the car or pram, sometimes at home, and often well into the afternoon.

I gently introduced the idea of a "flexible rhythm" — not a rigid schedule, but a predictable pattern that helped Liam's body and brain anticipate what was coming next.

We started with small changes: waking at the same time each morning (even if the night was rough), anchoring the first nap of the day, and placing more structure around meals. Within a week, Ava started to notice something surprising: Liam was calmer. He began showing clearer tired signs at more consistent times and settling for naps with less resistance.

Two weeks later, Liam was only waking once during the night, and Ava described bedtime as "peaceful — like we're both finally on the same page." But even more than the sleep improvements, Ava noticed that the entire day felt smoother. "It's like Liam is more settled in himself," she told me. "And I feel more confident knowing what's coming next, too."

This family's story is a powerful example of how rhythms — not rigid routines, but thoughtful, repeatable patterns — support a child's developing circadian system, reduce stress, and create a foundation for sleep and emotional regulation. Predictability isn't boring — it's soothing.

In Chapter 8, we'll begin exploring the third rung of the Ladder of Sleep Support: **Responsive Transitions**.

We'll look at:

- How to reduce sleep associations without distress

- The role of presence, fading, and comfort during change

- Practical strategies for slowly stepping back while keeping connection strong

Because sometimes, the way to more independent sleep starts with staying close — until your child is ready to let go.

Chapter 8

Responsive Transitions
Staying Present While Supporting Gentle Sleep Independence

You may have heard that babies and young children need to "learn to fall asleep on their own."
 And it's true — but not in the way many mainstream methods suggest.

In reality, **soothing independently is a developmental process**, shaped by nervous system maturity, trust, temperament, and experience. It's not a skill we can *teach* by stepping back abruptly — but it is a process we can *support*, gently and responsively.

In this chapter, we introduce the third rung of the Ladder of Sleep Support: **Responsive Transitions** — the in-between stage where your presence and support remain available, but you begin to gradually reduce how much you're doing to help your child fall asleep.

This is where many attachment-informed families make their biggest gains. It's where co-regulation slowly makes space for self-regulation — without harsh withdrawal or crying alone.

Why Responsive Transitions Matter

Babies who have always been rocked, fed, held, or co-slept to sleep are not doing anything wrong. In fact, those strategies are often what worked — and they helped your child feel safe enough to rest.

But over time, if those supports become unsustainable (or sleep disruptions emerge), some families begin to wonder:

- *Can we still respond… while also stepping back?*

- *How can we reduce night wakings without withdrawing comfort?*

Responsive transitions offer a path between two extremes:
  Doing everything for your child; and
  Leaving them to "figure it out" alone

Instead, you stay close — but adjust your role over time, gently and intentionally.

The Role of Sleep Associations

Let's quickly revisit the concept of **sleep associations**. These are the cues or behaviours a child relies on to fall asleep — like:

- Feeding to sleep

- Rocking or bouncing

- Being patted or sung to

- A parent lying beside them

- A specific toy, dummy, or blanket

- White noise, darkness, or routine

Sleep associations aren't bad. We all have them. But some are more sustainable than others. You may pause and reflect on your own sleep associations; do you doze off with the tv on, do you have a warm cup of tea in bed, a bit of white noise in the background, or do you drift off with a book, do you need a certain pillow in a certain position, or a blanket just the right weight hugging your body. We focus here on **external-to-internal** transitions. That means helping a child move from relying on external supports (rocking, feeding, touching) to internal cues (rubbing their comforter, turning onto their side, listening to white noise, or relaxing into your calming presence from a distance).

Common Responsive Transition Techniques

These approaches are grounded in *emotional safety*, not abandonment. You remain available and attuned, but start to shift *how* and *when* you offer support.

Here are some of the most widely used:

Parental Presence (a.k.a. Stay and Support)

You remain with your child as they fall asleep, offering soothing through:

- Touch

- Voice

- Eye contact

- Physical proximity

Over time, you reduce the intensity or frequency of support — perhaps switching from stroking to resting your hand, then just being nearby.

Example:
Week 1: Sit beside the cot, patting gently
Week 2: Sit beside the cot with just your voice
Week 3: Sit 1 metre away, offering occasional verbal reassurance
Week 4: Sit at the doorway, checking in every few minutes

Fading

Fading involves gradually reducing the time, intensity, or presence of sleep support — while allowing your child to adjust incrementally.

You might fade:

- The duration of rocking or patting

- The amount of milk before sleep

- The time spent lying next to your child

- The distance you are from the bed

This method is especially effective with toddlers and preschoolers who benefit from routines but resist abrupt changes.

Camping Out (Gradual Withdrawal)

Sometimes called "camping out" this involves gradually increasing your distance from your child over time — while still staying emotionally present.

This is often used after co-sleeping or bed-sharing transitions. For example:

- Start by sitting on the bed

- Then move to a chair beside the bed

- Then to the end of the bed

- Then outside the door

Always return to a closer step temporarily if your child struggles with the new position — it's a ladder, not an escalator.

Transitional Objects and Verbal Cues

Many children benefit from having:

- A consistent **comforter** (like a teddy, soft cloth, or item with your scent)

- A **mantra phrase** ("It's sleep time now, I'll stay with you")

- A **song or hum** that becomes a sleep cue over time

- A **"goodnight" routine** that includes a countdown or visual schedule

These tools help your child *internalise* the cues they need — moving from needing your physical action to finding comfort in familiar rhythms.

Adapting to Temperament

Some children transition smoothly. Others need more time.

It's helpful to consider:

- **Sensory sensitivity**: Does your child get overstimulated by touch or voice? Or do they need more sensory input to feel grounded?

- **Separation anxiety**: Are you transitioning during a developmental leap or big life change (e.g. starting daycare, a new sibling)?

- **Parent readiness**: Are you emotionally ready to stay regulated through the change?

There's no rush. In fact, pushing forward too fast often creates setbacks. It's okay to camp out on one step for weeks if it's working.

The Role of Repair

Even the most responsive transitions can involve protest.

That doesn't mean you've done it wrong. It means your child is noticing a change — and expressing themselves.

What matters most is what comes *after*.

Repair sounds like:

- "That was hard for you last night, wasn't it?"

- "You didn't like when I sat in the chair instead of the bed — but I was still with you."

- "You were upset, and I heard you. I'm here now. I always come back."

Repair rebuilds safety and reinforces that even when change is hard, the relationship remains steady.

Responsive, Not Reactive

The goal of responsive transitions isn't to prevent all emotion. It's to show your child:

> "You can feel big feelings — and I will stay calm, kind, and connected."

That's the secret to building emotional flexibility *and* sleep independence.

It's not the absence of tears that tells us a sleep plan is gentle — it's the presence of *attuned connection* during and after.

In Chapter 9, we'll explore the final rung of the ladder: **Behavioural Interventions** — and how they can be integrated with attachment principles when used with care and clarity.

We'll look at:

- What behavioural sleep strategies actually are

- How to use them in emotionally attuned ways

- When they're helpful — and when they're not

Because being attachment-informed doesn't mean avoiding all structure. It means delivering structure with sensitivity.

Responsive Transitions. It helps parents reflect on their own readiness, their child's temperament, and the possibilities of staying connected while gently stepping back.

Parent Reflection:

Take a quiet moment to reflect on the role *you* currently play in your child's falling asleep — and how that might evolve gently over time.

1. What sleep associations does my child currently rely on?

Do I rock, feed, lie beside them, or soothe them in other ways? What's working — and what's not?

2. How do I feel about making changes to those patterns?

Am I ready? Hesitant? Tired but unsure where to start?

3. How does my child tend to respond to change?

Are they flexible and curious, or cautious and reactive? How might I adjust my pace to match their needs?

4. What does "staying connected while stepping back" look like in our home?

Is it sitting nearby, singing a familiar song, using a comfort item — or simply offering presence without touch?

5. What small step toward independence feels right for us this week?

Could I reduce how long I stay, or shift from patting to just resting my hand? Could we try a "ladder" approach?

Chapter 9

Gentle Sleep Strategies That Respect Connection

When we think about sleep training, what usually comes to mind is crying—lots of it—and methods that leave many parents feeling uneasy, or worse, misaligned with their own values. But the truth is, there's a whole world of sleep strategies that don't require harshness or separation. These gentler methods don't just support sleep—they respect your baby's need for closeness and your intuition as a parent. In this chapter, we'll walk through a collection of responsive, emotionally-attuned techniques that may suit your family better than mainstream approaches.

Let's begin with one of the most well-known gentle sleep ideas: the Pantley Pull-Off.

The Pantley Pull-Off

Elizabeth Pantley's approach, from her book *The No-Cry Sleep Solution*, has been a staple in gentle parenting circles for years. One of the key techniques is the "Pantley Pull-Off." If you're breastfeeding to sleep but want to slowly shift that association, this method gives you a soft, responsive way to do so.

Here's how it works:

- You nurse your baby as usual.

- As they start to drift off and their sucking slows, you gently remove your nipple.

- They'll likely root again—so you try gently holding their chin closed with a finger or thumb.

- If they protest, you latch them again, count to ten, and try the pull-off again.

It's a bit like a gentle dance, repeated over and over until one night, your baby lets go without resistance and drifts off in your arms. Are they still almost asleep by then? Probably. But the real win is that over time, they start to get used to falling asleep *without* the nipple in their mouth.

Pantley's book also outlines a phased plan:

1. Comfort your baby until they're *almost* asleep, then place them down and hold them until they drift off.

2. Comfort them until drowsy, then place them down and just pat.

3. Try to avoid picking them up—just use patting or touch, and revert if needed.

4. Shift to minimal touch—just a few pats if they need them.

5. Stay in the doorway and use your voice for reassurance.

6. Eventually, you move outside the door, out of view.

At every phase, the parent responds immediately to crying. This isn't about timed intervals or shutting the door and crossing fingers. It's about helping baby sleep in a way that gradually builds their independence—without removing your presence or love.

Pantley writes, "Newborn babies do not have a sleep problem, but their parents do." And it's true—babies don't see their sleep habits as an issue. But we live in a world where rest is precious and often rare, and the mismatch between baby's needs and adult life can feel overwhelming. Her phased approach is a gentle way to bridge that gap.

The French "La Pause"

Another method that's gained popularity is what's known as *La Pause*—named for the French parenting style that encourages a small pause before responding to a baby's cry. According to parenting folklore, many French babies sleep through the night by 8–9 weeks. (Of course, this is a generalisation—not a prescription.)

The idea behind La Pause is to wait a few moments—maybe five minutes—before jumping out of bed. That time gives baby the chance to self-settle, wriggle back to sleep, or even find a thumb. If they don't settle, of course you respond. But the pause itself invites a more relaxed, observational style of parenting.

Now, let's be honest. Some of us are wired like caffeine-charged meerkats, leaping out of bed the moment we hear a whimper. Others (*ahem*, partners) somehow sleep through the apocalypse. La Pause encourages us to pause the automatic reaction—not to ignore baby, but to trust that a few moments might give them the space to resettle.

That said, for babies under 4 to 6 months who are likely waking due to hunger, it's wise not to pause too long. If the sound is more than a tired whimper, don't wait—go to them.

For those little sleep noises, though, you can wait a minute. If the noise stops, start the minute again. No timers, just trust and observation.

Crying in Arms

For those familiar with Aware Parenting, Dr. Aletha Solter's "Crying in Arms" method is an emotionally rich approach to sleep. Instead of nursing to sleep, the idea is to meet your baby's emotional needs through loving presence—*not* by trying to stop the crying, but by allowing it to be expressed in your arms.

Here's how it works:

- You feed your baby earlier in the evening.

- Go through your brief bedtime routine.

- Then simply hold them, lovingly, until they fall asleep.

If your baby needs to cry, they will. Offer water if needed, but avoid using the breast to soothe. According to Solter, the crying may be a release of stored emotions. Your role is to stay calm, present, and loving—not to stop the crying, but to be a safe container for it.

Sometimes, the cry is short. Other times, it takes longer. But many parents who use this approach find their babies begin sleeping better within a week and seem more peaceful during the day. Importantly, this method is *not* suitable for every family—especially not for parents who are feeling burnt out or overwhelmed. Holding a crying baby for an hour is emotionally and physically demanding, and if you're not in the right headspace, it's okay to choose something else.

It's also not suitable when baby doesn't need it. If your little one is instantly comforted or doesn't want to be held, then don't force it. Go with what they're telling you.

Montessori and Play-to-Sleep

Taking inspiration from Montessori parenting, the play-to-sleep approach involves giving a child some autonomy at bedtime. This might mean a mattress on the floor instead of a cot, or letting your toddler quietly play in bed until they're ready to sleep.

Sounds dreamy, right? But it also requires a lot of patience. This isn't the path to a 7 p.m. lights-out routine. It's more about following your child's rhythm and creating an environment that feels calm and safe—then letting them wind down at their own pace.

The key here is to watch for tired signs—but remember, hyperactivity is often a sign of *over*-tiredness. Many parents misread this as "they're not tired yet," when actually, it's the opposite. And while the freedom of this method sounds appealing, too much freedom too soon can lead to frustration on both sides if a young child doesn't yet have the self-regulation to stay put.

Still, for some families, especially those who value independence and don't mind an hour or two of quiet pre-sleep play, this can be a peaceful and enjoyable path.

Responsive Settling

Responsive settling is a common method used in Australian sleep schools. It's often described as a middle ground between controlled crying and more hands-on techniques.

Unlike strict interval-based methods, responsive settling asks parents to tune into the *type* of cry. Is baby shouting or truly distressed? If it's a shout, you might wait a little longer before responding. If it's a distressed cry, you go in.

But here's the rub: when you're sleep-deprived and emotionally drained, distinguishing cries can feel impossible. That's where frustration kicks in—and where well-meaning plans fall apart.

Which brings us to a method I've developed and teach in my training program: Monitored Settling.

Monitored Settling: A Tailored Approach

Monitored settling builds on responsive settling but removes rigid rules. There are no fixed intervals. No hard lines about cuddling or picking up. Instead, the only goal is this: support your child in falling asleep without relying fully on feeding, rocking, or patting all the way to sleep. Unlike other structured methods, this approach allows parent to attend to baby in whichever manner is needed presently by ongoing monitoring of the situation.

It doesn't have to be perfect on night one. Especially if you're shifting from co-sleeping or feeding to sleep, the first few nights may still involve hands-on support. That's okay. What matters is that we're gently nudging things forward.

A tool that really helps here is the **crying scale**—a personalised guide parents create to help them decide what type of crying is tolerable and what calls for immediate comfort. It's empowering because it gives parents *permission* to respond in a way that feels right to them—not what a book or consultant demands.

Some nights, the baby may be doing a tired whinge and just needs space. Other nights, they need you close. Monitored settling asks: What's going on for this child, and how does the parent feel about it? And we adjust from there.

The beauty of this approach is its flexibility. It honours the uniqueness of every child—and every parent.

In the next chapter, we'll explore how to approach **night weaning** in a way that doesn't leave anyone in tears (including you). It's all about tuning into your child, reading the readiness signs, and creating a plan that works for your family. Let's keep going.

Chapter 10

Night Weaning Without Breaking the Bond

If you've ever Googled "when should my baby sleep through the night?" at 3 a.m. while clutching a cold cup of tea and a warm, nursing baby, you're in good company. Night weaning is one of the biggest sleep hurdles families face — not because it's medically complicated, but because it touches everything from attachment and expectations to exhaustion and identity.

The truth? There's no single answer. But in this chapter, we'll walk through some of the most common approaches to night weaning — and more importantly, how to adapt them in a way that fits your baby, your parenting style, and your emotional bandwidth.

Is My Baby Ready to Night Wean?

Let's get this out of the way early: no one can say with absolute certainty when *your* baby is ready to drop night feeds. We can look at the research and general guidelines — many health professionals agree that, from a nutritional standpoint, most babies don't *need* a night feed after about six months. But emotional readiness? That's a different story.

Some babies are still waking at 8, 9, or 12 months for feeds, and that doesn't mean anything is "wrong." It could mean they're in the habit of feeding to sleep. It could mean they need that closeness. It could just be where they're at developmentally. And for parents? It's okay to want to keep feeding at night. It's also okay to want to stop.

There's no gold medal for night weaning at six months — just a path that needs to work for your baby and your sanity.

Popular Night Weaning Approaches (And What to Watch For)

Here are some of the most talked-about methods, with thoughts on how to gently tailor them:

Cold Turkey

The quick fix. One night the feed is there, the next night it's gone. This might be suitable for older babies or toddlers, especially when the night feed has become a 2-minute snack more out of habit than hunger.

Pros:

- Fast if it works.

- Can be easier for some parents to stick to one big change rather than gradual adjustments.

Cons:

- Can be emotionally intense for both baby and parent.

- May feel too abrupt, especially for sensitive little ones or parents who value connection in transitions.

- Not suitable under 9–12 months unless other conditions are met.

Sensitive sleep tip: If you're doing cold turkey, make sure you're replacing the feed with connection, not withdrawal. One parent might stay with the baby, offering touch, reassurance, or singing, so the baby knows they're not abandoned — just adjusting.

The Core Method

This method is based on identifying the longest stretch your baby *can* sleep without feeding (e.g., 6 hours), and committing to not offering feeds during that core block — then gradually stretching that window over time.

Pros:

- Logical.

- Baby's existing capacity guides the plan.

Cons:

- Confusing for baby — they don't know it's "not feed time yet."

- Can increase frustration if baby wakes and can't predict the response.

Sensitive sleep tip: I don't tend to recommend this approach as a standalone method, because it's not always obvious to the baby why things have changed. There's also a risk of overcomplicating things for already sleep-deprived parents. But if parents love a data-driven approach and their baby is thriving, it can be adapted with emotional support built in.

The Phased-Out Method (My Favourite)

This is the most flexible, responsive, and connection-preserving method of the bunch — and one I often recommend, especially for babies under 12 months.

Here's how it works:

You gradually reduce the length of each night feed over a period of nights, until the feed is minimal or gone altogether. For example:

- Night 1: feed for 15 minutes

- Night 2: 13 minutes

- Night 3: 11 minutes
  ... and so on.

Eventually, when you're down to just a couple of minutes, your baby is still awake after feeding and is gently learning to fall asleep without being fed all the way through.

Pros:

- Baby barely notices the change.

- Gives you time to assess and adapt as needed.

- Keeps the connection strong.

Cons:

- Takes longer than other methods.

- Requires consistency and patience — which can be tough in the middle of the night.

Sensitive sleep tip: Once you're down to just a minute or two, you can offer a cuddle instead of a feed. Some families like to offer water at this point, so baby doesn't feel they're waking for nothing — but also learns it's not worth waking for just water and a snuggle.

Extra Tips for a Smoother Night Weaning Transition

Some practical ways to make things easier (and kinder) for everyone:

- **Cover up** during the night. Whether it's doing up your bra properly, turning away from your baby, or wearing a shirt — reducing access helps signal the change.

- **Communicate** — even to babies. Say, "Boobies go night-night now. We'll feed again when the sun comes up." You'd be surprised how well they start to get it.

- **Bring in the other parent.** Dad or the non-feeding parent can take over the resettling role for a few nights. Sometimes the absence of milk is enough to break the habit.

- **Reduce bottle quantities** — if bottle feeding, try gradually reducing the volume in night bottles or watering them down.

- **Try feeding upright.** Sit in a chair rather than nursing in bed — helps avoid sleepy, snacky feeds.

- **Offer substitutes.** Dummies, soft toys, even a parent's hair (gently, we hope) — some babies just need that sensory cue to settle.

- **Tank them up during the day.** Full bellies and full love tanks help overnight.

Dr. Sears & Attachment-Informed Weaning

Dr. William Sears and his wife, Martha, have long been champions of attachment parenting — and they're clear that crying is not always the enemy. A baby crying in the arms of a loving parent is *not* the same as crying it out alone. They encourage us to listen, respond, and make room for emotion while still gently guiding change.

So yes — your baby might fuss or cry when you reduce a feed or when Daddy settles them instead of you. But that's not failure. That's transition. If they're held, heard, and supported, it's not abandonment — it's growth.

What About Co-Sleeping?

Many traditional sleep training methods weren't designed for co-sleeping families, but that doesn't mean you can't adapt them.

- You might start night weaning while still co-sleeping, and transition to independent sleep later.

- Or you might keep co-sleeping, but reduce feeds gradually.

- If you want to stop nursing to sleep, start by reducing feed times while keeping the cuddles.

- Respect the rhythm of your family — co-sleeping isn't a problem unless it *feels* like one for you.

Manage Expectations — With Compassion

It's important to remind yourself (and your partner or well-meaning relatives) that night weaning isn't always a magic bullet for sleep. Your baby might still wake for comfort, for connection, or just out of habit.

But if you're ready to reduce night feeds, and you want to do it in a way that's gentle, responsive, and emotionally attuned — then you're already on the right path.

This isn't about pushing your baby away. It's about guiding them into a new stage of growth, with you right beside them.

Final Thoughts: Night Weaning as an Act of Love

Night weaning isn't about withholding love — it's about reshaping how love and comfort are offered during the night. For some babies, that shift is smooth. For others, it's messy, emotional, and full of mixed signals. But for all babies, what matters most is *how* you do it — not how quickly, not how perfectly, but how connected you stay through the process.

So if you're holding a baby who's crying because they want to feed, and you're gently saying, "I'm here, I love you, but we're going to do this differently now" — that's not letting them down. That's showing up. That's parenting in the tension between comfort and change.

Remember: you are not just teaching your child how to sleep — you're teaching them that change can happen in the context of safety, closeness, and love.

Take your time. Trust your instincts. And know that you don't have to get it right every night to get it right overall.

Chapter 11:

Behavioural Interventions — *Building Structure Without Breaking Connection*

In this chapter, we explore how behavioural sleep strategies can be used in an attachment-safe and emotionally attuned way. This includes understanding when and how to use strategies like fading, parental presence, timed check-ins, or structured sleep coaching plans — without undermining the child's felt safety or emotional development.

Making Sense of Sleep Training: What Behavioural Science Actually Says

When parents hear the words *sleep training*, strong feelings usually bubble up. Some imagine long nights of leaving babies to cry alone. Others think of elaborate sticker charts or strict bedtime schedules. And many simply feel conflicted — torn between wanting more sleep and wanting to protect their child's sense of safety.

But here's the thing: sleep training isn't one rigid method. At its core, it's a set of behavioural strategies designed to change how children fall asleep and return to sleep during the night. And when we peel back the myths and jargon, what we find is that behavioural sleep strategies can be used gently, flexibly, and — most importantly — in ways that protect the bond you share with your child.

This chapter will take you behind the curtain of behavioural science and explain what's really going on when we talk about "sleep training." You'll learn the principles in plain language, see how the different methods actually work, and understand how to judge whether they're the right fit for your family.

What Behaviour Modification Actually Means

The foundation of most sleep training methods is something called *behaviour modification*. It sounds clinical, but it simply means changing a behaviour (in this case, sleep patterns) by changing what happens before, during, or after it.

In psychology, behaviours are strengthened or weakened by what follows them. This is called **reinforcement**.

- If a behaviour is followed by something pleasant, it's more likely to happen again.

- If it's followed by something unpleasant — or nothing at all — it's less likely to be repeated.

When applied to sleep, the "behaviour" is how your child falls asleep and what they expect during the night. If they usually fall asleep in your arms and wake expecting the same comfort, they'll cry until they get it. If the conditions change — and they learn that falling asleep happens in their cot, with you nearby but not holding them — then over time, their expectations shift.

This is the psychology behind sleep training. It's not about tricking children or ignoring their needs. It's about helping them link sleep with new cues that they can access more independently.

Core Principles of Behavioural Sleep Strategies

Before we look at the specific methods, it's worth understanding the basic principles at work:

1. **Consistency is key**
   Children thrive on predictable patterns. If the response is different every night, they don't know what to expect — and their protests can actually intensify.

2. **Extinction (with variations)**
   Extinction in psychology means reducing a behaviour by removing what usually reinforces it. In sleep training, this often refers to gradually reducing how much hands-on help a child receives at bedtime. (Don't worry — we'll unpack this in detail soon.)

3. **Graduation, not shock**
   Behaviour change usually works best when it's gradual. That's why many modern approaches use "stepped" methods rather than cold-turkey changes.

4. **Parental presence matters**
   Studies often overlook the *emotional tone* of how sleep strategies are done. A parent who stays calm, present, and reassuring can make a huge difference, even if they're slowly reducing hands-on settling.

5. **Temperament changes everything**
   A laid-back child may adapt quickly to changes. A highly sensitive child may need more steps, more reassurance, and a gentler approach. One-size-fits-all plans rarely work in the real world.

The Main Sleep Training Interventions

Now let's walk through the most common behavioural sleep strategies, from the most structured to the gentler, parent-friendly adaptations.

1. Extinction (a.k.a. "Cry It Out")

This is the most controversial method — and also the least commonly recommended today. Extinction means placing your child in bed, saying goodnight, and not returning until morning (except for safety or illness).

How it works:

- The crying isn't reinforced by parental attention, so it gradually reduces.

- Children eventually learn to fall asleep without needing external help.

Why it's hard:

- For most parents, listening to prolonged crying feels unbearable.

- Sensitive children may escalate rather than settle.

- Without reassurance, some families report emotional stress or worsened bedtime battles.

My take: While some families do use this method, I rarely recommend it in its pure form. It doesn't sit well with attachment-informed care and can easily cross into emotional disconnection.

2. Graduated Extinction (Controlled Comforting / Controlled Crying)

This is the method many people think of when they hear "sleep training." Instead of leaving a child indefinitely, parents check in at set intervals.

How it works:

- You place your child in bed awake.

- If they cry, you wait a set time before returning to comfort briefly.

- The intervals gradually increase — for example, 2 minutes, then 5, then 10.

- Comfort is brief and not designed to re-settle the child fully.

Why it helps:

- The child learns that while parents are nearby, they won't always step in immediately.

- Over time, the child develops more self-settling skills.

Limitations:

- Still involves crying, which many parents find stressful.

- Can escalate distress in sensitive or anxious children.

- Requires consistency — chopping and changing often backfires.

My take: Controlled comforting can work for some children, especially those who cope well with boundaries. But it's not for everyone. Parents need to feel emotionally okay with the process, and children need enough regulation capacity to handle it.

3. Camping Out (The Presence Method)

Camping out involves staying in the room with your child as they learn to fall asleep, and then gradually reducing your involvement over time.

How it works:

- You sit or lie near your child's bed, offering comfort through presence.

- Over nights or weeks, you slowly move further away — from sitting beside the cot, to near the door, to outside the room.

- The child falls asleep with reassurance that you're close, but with less hands-on settling each step.

Why it helps:

- Reduces separation anxiety.

- Allows children to practice falling asleep in their own sleep space while still feeling safe.

- Gives parents flexibility — you can linger longer on harder nights, or move faster on easier ones.

Limitations:

- Can take longer to "work" than extinction methods.

- Parents sometimes get stuck at one stage (e.g., still sitting beside the bed months later).

My take: Camping out is one of the most attachment-friendly behavioural strategies. It honours the child's need for safety while gently building independent sleep skills.

4. Parental Presence with Hands-On Settling Adjustments

Some methods involve continuing to help your child fall asleep, but in gradually reduced ways.

Examples include:

- **Pick up/put down:** Lifting the baby when upset, then putting them back down once calm. Repeated as many times as needed.

- **Hands-on settling:** Patting, shushing, or stroking while the baby is in bed, then reducing the intensity over time.

- **The Pantley Pull-Off:** Allowing a baby to nurse to sleep, then gently removing the nipple before they're fully asleep — slowly increasing the time they can stay settled without feeding.

Why it helps:

- Keeps parents highly responsive.

- Works well for sensitive children and parents who dislike crying-based approaches.

- Creates a step-by-step bridge between full support and independent sleep.

Limitations:

- Can take longer to see results.

- Requires patience and persistence.

- Risk of reverting if parents return to full settling at the first hurdle.

My take: These are excellent "middle ground" strategies. They're especially useful for parents who want to preserve closeness but also need a pathway out of hours-long rocking, feeding, or patting.

5. The Gentle Steps Approach

Think of this as a flexible framework rather than a strict method. The idea is to visualise sleep support as a staircase:

- The bottom steps are full parental support (feeding to sleep, rocking, lying beside).

- The higher stepss are semi-supportive (hands-on settling, presence, comfort from a distance).

- The top steps are independent sleep.

Parents can decide where on the staircase to begin, and move up or down depending on how their child is coping.

Why it helps:

- Provides flexibility.

- Recognises that progress isn't linear — some nights you may need to "climb back down" for more support.

- Encourages parents to celebrate small wins, not just complete independence.

Bringing It All Together

Sleep training isn't one rigid recipe. It's a menu of strategies, all built on the principles of behaviour modification. Some are quick but tough, others are slower but gentler. None are inherently "good" or "bad" — what matters is how they're used, whether they suit your child's temperament, and whether they align with your family's values.

The heart of attachment-friendly sleep work is this: **you can support healthy sleep without breaking the bond.**

As you read on, you'll see how these methods can be adapted, softened, or combined into a plan that feels both effective and emotionally safe.

In the next chapter, we'll take these methods off the page and into real life. You'll see how they look in practice, how to adapt them to your child, and how to set limits gently but firmly — without ever losing connection.

Why Behavioural Interventions Are Often Misunderstood

When parents hear the term *sleep training*, many instinctively react with discomfort — associating it with harsh or rigid methods like controlled crying or "cry-it-out." And for good reason: used carelessly, behavioural strategies can ignore emotional cues, escalate distress, and harm a child's sense of safety.

But behavioural interventions, when modified through the lens of attachment theory, can instead offer consistency, clarity, and confidence — for both child and parent. The key lies not in whether we use structure, but in how we deliver it.

The most effective sleep support is a balanced approach that considers:

○ The **child's temperament and developmental stage**.

○ **Respectful responsiveness** to crying (comforting or allowing space, as appropriate).

○ An approach that **does not rigidly rely on timed checks** but is adaptable and emotionally attuned.

These interventions aim to help children develop the ability to fall asleep and return to sleep independently — a process called *self-settling*. Not to be confused with *self-soothing* (which implies regulating emotions without support), *self-settling* is a physiological skill that babies and children can gradually develop with guidance and support.

Key Considerations Before Introducing Sleep Strategies

Before implementing a behavioural intervention, consider the following:

- Is the child developmentally ready for this approach?

- Has the family already established strong foundations (e.g., routines, emotional safety, appropriate sleep associations)?

- Are the caregivers emotionally regulated and resourced enough to follow through consistently?

- Are there any health or neurodevelopmental factors (e.g. reflux, autism, ADHD) that need to be taken into account?

- Is the child's environment supportive of restful sleep (e.g. temperature, light, diet)?

The Ladder of Sleep Support: Matching Intervention to Readiness

In earlier chapters, we introduced the **Ladder of Sleep Support** — a framework for gradually increasing a child's independence at sleep time. This ladder helps families identify where they are currently at, and which next small step is appropriate.

The key is to *never climb faster than the child can emotionally manage*, and to ensure each step remains relational and responsive.

Using Interventions Within an Attachment-Friendly Framework

When behavioural strategies are used in a way that maintains attunement, responsiveness, and co-regulation, they can be powerful tools for change.

Here's how:

- **Be emotionally available throughout** — even if you're not in the room, stay responsive to your child's cues, cries, or calls.

- **Narrate what's happening** — tell your child what you're doing and why: "I'm here to help you learn to sleep. I'll be nearby."

- **Use a calming pre-bedtime ritual** that fills your child's cup with connection.

- **Track progress gently** — avoid rigid timelines. Look for gradual improvements in ease of settling and reduced need for intervention.

- **Allow room to pause** — if your child becomes distressed beyond their window of tolerance, scale back, and re-establish emotional safety.

A Note on Crying and Cortisol

There's a lot of fear around crying and cortisol. While prolonged, unbuffered crying can lead to elevated stress responses, *not all crying is harmful*. In fact, crying *with support* can be a way of processing change and distress.

The focus shouldn't be to eliminate crying, but to *respond to it in ways that preserve connection*. Children can learn to settle while experiencing manageable levels of protest, especially when they know they're not alone.

Rhythm & Routine Support

Best suited for: newborns and young infants, families avoiding any "training", or as a first step before formal methods.

This approach focuses on:

- Creating predictable sequences (cue–routine–sleep)

- Protecting naps, nutrition, and wake windows

- Managing stimulation and transitions

- Calming nervous system input via soothing routines

There's no attempt to teach settling at this stage — just to shape the conditions that make settling possible over time.

Why it works:
This method supports the development of self-regulation and sleep rhythms without any pressure. It's also ideal for families who are sleep-deprived but not ready for behavioural change.

Supported Settling (Co-regulation Methods)

Best suited for: infants and toddlers who need parental support to fall asleep or transition between sleep cycles.

This approach focuses on:

- Rocking, patting, cuddling, or vocal soothing until drowsy/asleep

- Responding consistently to night wakes with in-arms or in-crib comfort

- Using calming cues (voice, scent, rhythm, presence)

Often used in combination with gentle fade-out techniques over time.

Why it works:
It honours attachment needs, allows the child to feel emotionally safe, and supports sensitive transitions. It's also aligned with the principles of responsive parenting and attachment theory.

Common method types:

- Pick-up-put-down

- Hands-on settling

- Chair settling while holding presence

Parental Presence / Fading

Best suited for: toddlers and older infants who rely on strong parental input but may be developmentally ready to learn new sleep associations.

This approach uses:

- A clear routine

- Calm connection at bedtime

- Gradual reduction of physical or verbal input over days or weeks

Examples include:

- Sitting beside the cot/bed and gradually moving further away (camping out)

- Reducing the length of cuddling or patting over time

- Introducing comfort objects as transitional tools

Why it works:
 It allows for emotional support while gently promoting

more independent sleep. Parents feel more confident because they are present and involved.

Key reminder:
 Progress can be slow but steady. Emotional connection is never removed — only reshaped.

Independent Sleep Conditioning

Best suited for: older infants or toddlers (usually 6+ months) where all other shaping and support strategies have been tried, and where parents feel informed and ready.

These may include but not limited to:

- Interval-based reassurance (brief visits at increasing intervals)

- Positive reinforcement systems for older toddlers

Why it works:
 In some cases, structured behavioural interventions can reduce confusion and support a more rapid transition to independent sleep. However, they must always be offered with full explanation, careful emotional support, and alignment with the family's values.

Important:
 At our Institute, these methods are *implored collectively and collaboratively*, sensitively — with plenty of space for repair and adaptation.

Adapting Sleep Support for Bedsharing Families

Very importantly, I'd like to add, that we specialise in maintaining a family's values - and that certainly includes supporting their wish to keep the family bed. Many families choose to bedshare, either intentionally from birth or as a survival strategy during challenging sleep phases. Sensitive Sleep Consultants do not view bedsharing as incompatible with healthy sleep — rather, we see it as one of many approaches that can be supported with intentionality, safety, and consistency. Whilst we promote Safe Sleep, which involves placing baby in an independent sleep space, we can also work with safe ways of co-sleeping, and informing parents of risk.

When a family wishes to <u>continue bedsharing</u> but improve sleep, the focus shifts toward:

- Establishing predictable pre-sleep routines (even within the shared space)

- Encouraging independent settling while in proximity — such as teaching the child to fall asleep beside a calm, resting parent rather than relying on feeding, rocking, or movement

- Using verbal cues, rhythm, and gentle boundary-setting (e.g., hands-off soothing, decreasing physical contact as sleep begins)

- Transitioning from contact-dependent sleep to co-regulated but less interactive settling

- Making incremental changes like starting the night in the shared bed and moving to a floor mattress if needed for space or safety

Sleep teaching within a bedsharing framework is absolutely possible — and when approached with attunement and consistency, it can promote longer stretches of rest without undermining the closeness and responsiveness that many families value.

Sensitive consultants don't pressure families to move babies to a cot if that's not aligned with their parenting style. Instead, we adapt the principles of rhythm, responsiveness, and behavioural science *within* the family's chosen arrangement. Our consultants are encouraged to include a disclaimer upon engagement with a family that includes educating on risk of bedsharing with young infants.

Matching Methods to Families

No two families are the same. Choosing a method requires considering:

- The child's age, temperament, feeding and health needs

- Parental capacity, values, and trauma history

- Cultural expectations and support systems

- Emotional readiness for change

Sleep work is relational — not mechanical. What works for one family may not feel right for another.

Combining Methods Creatively

Sometimes a hybrid approach works best. For example:

- A toddler may start with a strong rhythm routine and then shift into presence-based fading

- An infant may benefit from hands-on settling at bedtime and more responsive feeding overnight

- A parent might begin with pick-up-put-down and then move into chair-based settling

Camping Out (Parental Presence)

Overview:
A gradual method where a parent stays in the room and offers physical or verbal reassurance as the child falls asleep, then slowly increases space between themselves and the child over time.

Best suited for:
Children used to falling asleep with a parent right next to them or in the bed.

Attachment-Friendly Steps:

1. Start with your usual bedtime routine.

2. Sit beside your child's bed. Offer touch or calming voice as needed.

3. Once your child can fall asleep consistently with you beside them, shift the chair 30cm away.

4. Continue gradually moving further away every few nights — only as your child shows comfort.

5. Eventually, aim for sitting at the doorway, and then outside the door if needed.

Parent Tip:
Bring a quiet activity like knitting or a book to keep yourself relaxed. Your calm presence sets the tone.

Timed Check-Ins (Modified Graduated Extinction)

Overview:
Parent leaves the room and returns at set intervals to offer brief reassurance. Modified to reduce child distress and maintain emotional safety.

Best suited for:
Children who benefit from routine, predictability, and brief reassurance rather than continuous presence.

Attachment-Friendly Steps:

1. Finish the bedtime routine with extra connection (story, cuddle, prayer/blessing, etc.).

2. Tell your child you'll check in on them — and **follow through** reliably.

3. Step out for 1–2 minutes. Return to check in briefly — a calm "I'm right here, it's sleep time now" — no picking up or re-engaging in conversation.

4. Gradually increase time between check-ins as your child shows signs of settling.

5. Maintain warmth and consistency, not pressure.

Parent Tip:
Use a visual check-in card or nightlight countdown to help your child feel secure between check-ins.

The Chair Method (Gradual Withdrawal)

Overview:

Similar to Camping Out, but focused on reducing verbal/physical input slowly while staying nearby.

Best suited for:

Children who respond to proximity more than direct touch or interaction.

Attachment-Friendly Steps:

1. Sit in a chair right by your child's bed. No touching, but offer a few words of reassurance as needed. Feel free to use soft eye contact and calming voice.

2. Over several nights, reduce how often you speak.

3. After 3–5 nights, move the chair slightly away.

4. Repeat the process — staying emotionally available, but gradually reducing input.

Parent Tip:

Practice affirmations: "They are safe, I am present, they are learning something new."

Pick-Up, Put-Down Method

Overview:
This method allows parents to respond to distress by picking the baby up to calm them and then placing them back in the cot once calm — repeating as needed.

Best suited for:
Babies aged 3–9 months who need physical contact to calm but are learning to settle in their own space.

Attachment-Friendly Steps:

1. Wind down with a calming bedtime routine.

2. Place your baby in their cot drowsy but awake.

3. If they protest with rising distress, pick them up and hold until calm (not asleep).

4. Put them back down gently, with a soft voice: "It's sleep time, I'm right here."

5. Repeat as needed, aiming to gradually reduce pickups over time.

Parent Tip:

Stay tuned to your baby's signals. If crying escalates immediately after putting down, slow the pace — your baby is asking for more co-regulation.

Hands-On Settling (In-Cot Support)

Overview:
Gently soothing your child to sleep with your hands on their body (e.g., patting, stroking, firm still hand) while they lie in their sleep space.

Best suited for:
Babies and toddlers who are used to being rocked, fed, or held to sleep and are ready to try falling asleep in the cot.

Attachment-Friendly Steps:

1. Begin with a calm wind-down routine.

2. Place your child in the cot and stay close, placing a hand on their chest/back.

3. Use gentle, rhythmic touch (patting or stroking) and soft shushing or humming.

4. As nights progress, slowly reduce the intensity and frequency of input.

5. Eventually transition to placing your hand still, then just sitting nearby.

Parent Tip:
Breathe slowly and calmly. Your nervous system helps regulate theirs — let your touch say, "I'm right here, and you're safe."

Chair Settling with Holding Presence (Toddler and Older Child)

Overview:
This is a gentle sleep training option where the parent provides verbal and emotional presence from a chair nearby — particularly suited to toddlers and preschoolers who resist being alone but don't need physical contact.

Best suited for:
Children aged 2–5 who are capable of settling in bed with support but struggle with separation.

Attachment-Friendly Steps:

1. Complete your bedtime routine and tuck your child in.

2. Sit in a chair beside the bed. Offer short phrases of reassurance if needed (e.g., "I'm right here," "It's time to rest").

3. Feel free to use soft eye contact and calming voice.

4. Night by night, move the chair further away until you're out of the room.

5. Continue morning praise and connection to reinforce progress.

Parent Tip:
Some parents find a simple bedtime mantra (e.g., "We rest, we grow, we sleep") helps remind both adult and child that this is a learning journey, not a battle.

A Sample Attachment-Friendly Behavioural Plan

Let's say a family is ready to support their 10-month-old to fall asleep without being fed to sleep. Here's a simplified plan that uses **Parental Presence with Fading**:

1. **Night 1–3**: Parent lies next to cot, hand on baby until asleep.

2. **Night 4–6**: Parent sits next to cot, minimal touch, verbal reassurance.

3. **Night 7–10**: Parent moves chair halfway to door.

4. **Night 11–14**: Parent sits near door, minimal verbal reassurance.

5. **Night 15+**: Parent sits outside door, available if needed.

This is flexible, compassionate, and always reversible if the child becomes overwhelmed.

For Older Children

Behavioural interventions for preschoolers and beyond may include:

- Reward charts for staying in bed

- Bedtime passes

- Predictable bedtime routines

- Clear expectations and follow-through

- Night lights or comfort items

All strategies should be delivered with calm, consistency, and connection — never in anger or withdrawal.

Parent Reflection:

Most parents feel apprehensive about starting a new routine. Take a moment to explore for yourself what questions you might have ahead of going into this process.

"What's my biggest fear when it comes to sleep training?
Is it the fear of hearing my child cry?
Worrying they'll feel abandoned?
Or fearing I won't cope emotionally myself?
Now, imagine a version of sleep support that isn't harsh or rigid — but respectful, flexible, and grounded in connection.
What if sleep changes didn't mean 'leaving' my child, but gently showing them they can rest and feel safe, even with a little more space?
How might I approach things differently if I trusted that my presence — even when I'm not holding them — still brings comfort?
What does 'being with' my child look like, even when I'm supporting them to fall asleep on their own?"

Chapter 12

Gentle to Gradual: Finding the Right Fit for Your Family

By now you've seen that "sleep training" isn't one fixed method but a whole toolbox of behavioural strategies. The challenge for most parents isn't whether sleep training *works* — research tells us it usually does, at least in the short term. The real question is: *Which approach works for your child, in your family, in a way that you feel good about?*

This chapter brings those methods down to earth. Instead of theory or research summaries, you'll meet families who've walked the road — composites built from many real stories I've encountered. Each example shows how different parents adapted gentle through to more structured approaches, and how they navigated the balance between sleep and emotional connection.

Case One: The Gentle Shift — Emma and Baby Noah

Emma had a six-month-old, Noah, who would only sleep on the breast. She loved the closeness, but after hours of rocking, patting, and feeding every night, she was exhausted. Emma knew she wasn't ready for anything that involved tears. She wanted a plan that felt nurturing, even if it took longer.

We began with **hands-on settling**. Emma would feed Noah until he was drowsy, then lay him down and pat gently until he drifted off. At first, this still took ages — but Noah was learning that falling asleep could happen in his cot, not just on the breast.

Next, Emma tried the **Pantley Pull-Off** method: feeding Noah to sleepy, then gently slipping him off before he was fully asleep. If he fussed, she'd comfort and try again. It was slow going — weeks rather than days — but Emma noticed progress. Eventually, Noah was nursing less at night and falling asleep with just a pat and a cuddle.

For Emma, this approach worked because it matched her values. She felt she was still responding warmly to Noah's needs while also moving towards healthier sleep. Yes, it required patience, but Emma's confidence grew as Noah adapted gently and without distress.

Case Two: The Middle Ground — Liam and Toddler Sophie

Liam's daughter Sophie was 18 months old and fiercely independent during the day, but bedtime was another story. Sophie wanted one of her parents lying beside her until she was asleep — often for an hour or more. The family needed a change, but Liam and his partner didn't want to abandon Sophie to cry.

We started with the **Camping Out** method. Liam sat beside Sophie's cot, offering verbal reassurance and holding her hand. Over a week, he shifted his chair slightly further away each night. Sophie protested at first — "Daddy, come back!" — but she could still see him, and his calm presence helped her feel safe.

Soon Liam was sitting by the door, and then outside the door. By week three, Sophie was falling asleep without him in the room. There were tears, yes, but they were brief, and Sophie adjusted quickly with the security of her dad's calm reassurance.

For Liam, the beauty of this approach was that it respected Sophie's need for connection while setting clear boundaries. It was neither "all in" nor "all out" — just a middle ground that worked for their temperament as a family.

Case Three: When there's "a lot going on"

Becky is a content fourteen month old girl who had difficulty falling asleep independently and staying asleep at night, and difficulty at naptime. Her parents Jessica and Sally reported they attempted to implement controlled crying before 6 months of age, however, felt it was not suited to their parenting style. Jessica shared that in the last month she had attempted to put Becky down awake but she struggles. Jessica reported to me that around 5am they co-sleep in another room. Becky's parents indicated that she is learning to walk and possibly teething.

Sally shared that she is 31 weeks pregnant, and Becky appears aware of the news. Sally and Jessica indicated concerns with variable naps and multiple night wake ups for the past few months. Becky's history of sleep habits was explored from birth, with typical habits noted in the neonate period, and sleeping through the night from 8 months following a family holiday to Cairns. Around 10 months old, Becky began waking in the night again. Jessica was due to return to work part time in the coming weeks. Jessica also indicated she would like to teach Becky independent sleeping so that others can put her to bed easier in her absence.

With multiple elements within this case, such as upcoming changes in the family - one parent returning to work and the other due to give birth, Sally and Jessica felt pressure of looming deadlines to fix Becky's sleep before things got unmanageable. Jessica was worried that Sally would not be able to handle Becky on her own at bedtime and Sally was worried about having a newborn and toddler co-sleeping with her. My first job was to ease the parents. We spoke about expectation management and I suggested that we should consider breaking down the problem into manageable goals to work with, so that the parents could gain a sense of achievement / control of their situation. I encouraged them to be kind to themselves and eachother and remember that they are doing a good job supporting Becky and comforting her needs during this process.

Becky's plan included decreasing lights in the house and bedroom in the 30 minutes before bedtime so that Becky's body will signal the sleepy hormone melatonin to come in and activate her natural drive for sleep. Becky and parents could enjoy a cozy feed together in a dim-lit room.   When putting Becky into her cot, we anticipated that she would stand up and fuss, because she is going through an important developmental milestone; learning to walk. It is biologically appropriate that infants become obsessed with practicing their new skill, even at night. I suggested that Jessica should stay calm and be aware to not find herself continuously laying her down/ holding her down in the cot as she will be more upset and it will be either a battle or a game no body wins. I advised the parents that they should pick Becky up and cuddle or hold her (no rocking) when she is upset, until she is nice and calm and try again. If she looks like she's distressed, offer breastfeeding as this is a natural relaxer and encourages bonding/security. There is no limit to how many times you can cuddle your child! However, we tailored a plan that included how to pay attention to her body signals if she may be indicating frustration at being picked up and put down too often, and what to do if this is occuring.

By the time Jessica had to return to work, Sally had mastered the bedtime settling routine with Becky and she was going to sleep with minimal fuss, if at all. By the time Sally gave birth to Becky's brother, Becky was staying put in her own cot all night. Sally was pleased she could enjoy co-sleeping with the new baby without worrying about Becky in the bed too.

Case Four: Nightmares

Kian is a very active and happy 20 month old boy who has difficulty staying asleep and prolonged onset of sleep. Tracy reported the birth was somewhat difficult; however Kian appeared to be settled relatively well at home and does not display obvious traumatic response indicators. Tracy described a bit of a rough start in regards to not being able to pick him up due to recovering from her surgery complication. We also discussed how another period of separation anxiety is natural around this age 18-20 month olds. He is on track developmentally and meeting his milestones. His parents, Con and Tracy report Kian has a history of infections / anti biotics use related to enlarged tonsils. He was directed to sleep propped with a pillow as an infant, and there have been no significant issues with ceasing breathing in sleep.

Kian had nightmares or night terrors on occasion and we discussed ways to manage if they reoccur. He was sleeping okay around 13 months old (only one wake up on average), but sleep declined dramatically around 4 months ago with the bouts of infections. Con and Tracy indicated concerns with multiple wake ups in the night and prolonged return to sleep. Kian is able to settle himself to sleep with his pacifier at the beginning of bedtimes, but requires parental assistance during the night. He is currently still drinking some diluted milk at the wake ups. Tracy reports that Kian seems to have some difficulty self-regulating emotions, so for this reason we decided to not take away his pacifier at night at the moment.

Assessment of situation and history indicates his sleep issue is likely behavioural related now. Tracy and Con are fatigued and frustrated but are trying various coping strategies such as taking turns in caring duties and being mindful of stress in the home. They do not have a family network close by but an understanding employer (although they do worry about the impact of sleep deprivation on fulfilling their duties).

This approach required several phases. In our first phase I advised on making some slight changes, but ultimately trying to keep most of his usual routine in place so not to confuse or upset Kian.   The main changes in the first phase (one week) are:

- Experiment with removing TV watching from the bedtime routine for a week.

- For night time drinks, remove milk from bottle; just use plain water and cut the amount of liquid in half. Make sure Kian is getting enough milk during the day.
- Stay with Kian, patting firmly but slowly with his 'Sheepy' (a glowing lullaby toy). However, attempt to leave after 2 minutes (before the music stops).

Tracy has been elected as the main responder to wake ups, as Kian responds easier to her. Tracy was aware she could always comfort him and start over. It is OK if it takes many attempts in the initial phase. If he is upset, pick up and cuddle until calm and try again. If he looks like he's distressed at all, go in straight away.

The second phase involved a plan of how to phase-out Tracy's patting, and leaving the room a lot sooner. We trouble-shooted what to do if Kian was not settling after Tracy left the room. We also revisited teaching him to press Sheepy on himself, so he could play with this for comfort instead of calling out for a parent to press the button. Tracy and Con reported success within several weeks, and were pleased that nothing drastic or upsetting was implemented.

What These Stories Show Us

Each of these families chose differently — and each found a way forward. What mattered wasn't which method they picked, but how well it fit:

- **Emma** needed a gentle, low-stress approach.

- **Liam** needed a middle path that combined comfort with limits.

- **Becky** needed a phased approach to restore sleep quickly.

- **Kian** needed a holistic and soothing approach to regain his bedtime confidence after nightmares

None of these families "failed" or "succeeded" based on how long it took or whether their children slept through the night at a set age. Success was defined by finding balance: protecting the child's emotional safety while restoring the family's ability to rest.

Finding Your Fit

As you think about your own child, ask yourself:

- How sensitive is my child to change?

- How sensitive am *I* to crying?

- How urgently do we need better sleep?

- What values guide how I want to respond at night?

Your answers will point you towards an approach that feels doable, respectful, and sustainable. Remember — it's not about choosing the "best" method, but the best *fit*.

In the next chapters, we'll explore how special circumstances — like separation anxiety, neurodivergence and trauma shape sleep, and how to adjust strategies when sleep feels especially hard. But for now, take comfort in this: you don't have to follow a script. Sleep support isn't a pass-or-fail test. It's a journey of finding the pace, presence, and process that works for your unique child and family.

Chapter 13

The Neurodivergent Sleeper

ADHD, Autism, and Sensory Needs — Supporting Sleep Without Sacrificing Emotional Safety

Some kids don't fit the mould — and that includes the sleep mould.

You can read all the baby books, download all the visual charts, and set up a perfect bedtime routine... only to find your child still doing laps around the living room at 10 p.m., begging for "just one more spin" on the office chair while wearing a pair of noise-cancelling headphones and one sock.

Welcome to the world of neurodivergent sleep.

Whether your child has ADHD, autism, sensory processing differences, or is just more intense and complex in their wiring, this chapter is for you. Sleep advice that works for neurotypical children often backfires with neurodivergent ones — not because you're doing something wrong, but because these children require a different approach. One that honours their unique brains, their sensory experiences, and their deep need for both predictability and flexibility.

Understanding Neurodivergence and Sleep

Neurodivergence is an umbrella term that includes autism, ADHD, sensory processing differences, and other variations in brain development. These are not disorders to be fixed — they are different ways of experiencing and responding to the world. And that includes how a child experiences sleep.

Sleep is fundamentally a process of *regulation* — the nervous system needs to shift from active, alert states into rest and restoration. But for many neurodivergent children, this shift is far from seamless.

- Children with **ADHD** often experience *hyperarousal*, meaning their nervous system is revving like an engine that can't idle.

- Children with **autism** may have *hypersensitivities* (e.g., to light, noise, clothing) or *hyposensitivities* (e.g., needing more input before they feel tired).

- Many neurodivergent kids have **difficulty with transitions**, and bedtime is the ultimate daily transition — from busy to still, from connection to separation, from control to surrender.

The result? A bedtime routine that feels more like a battlefield than a wind-down.

Case Story: Max's Never-Ending Bedtime

Max was a seven-year-old with a recent autism diagnosis. His parents, Kate and Liam, came to me exhausted. "He just *won't* go to sleep," Kate said. "It takes two hours every night, and by the end we're all in tears."

Their routine was consistent — bath, book, bed — but Max would resist every step. The lights had to be just right. His blanket had to be placed "with the stars facing up." If Liam kissed him goodnight before Kate, he would yell and start again. Any deviation spiralled into a meltdown.

What was happening? Max was overloaded by the sensory and emotional demands of the day. His routine was visually predictable, but emotionally overwhelming. He needed more sensory input before calming, not less. He wasn't being difficult — he was *having* difficulty.

Unique Challenges — and Hidden Strengths

Neurodivergent kids often bring extraordinary creativity, sensitivity, and insight — but those same qualities can make sleep especially tricky.

Common challenges include:

- **Sensory processing issues** (too hot, too itchy, too loud, too tight)

- **Rigid thinking** (trouble when routines change or rules are broken)

- **Difficulty with emotional regulation** (big feelings at bedtime)

- **Delayed sleep phase** (some children's body clocks are naturally wired later)

- **Stimming** (repetitive behaviours that can increase before sleep)

But here's the flip side: these kids often thrive with the *right kind* of structure. One that provides safety without stifling, and flexibility without chaos.

Adapting Sleep Support — Gentle Structure for Intense Kids

A common misconception is that neurodivergent kids can't handle limits. In reality, they often crave them — as long as those limits are communicated clearly, upheld consistently, and supported compassionately.

The key is **gentle structure**. Here's what that looks like:

- **Predictable but not rigid** routines. Your bedtime routine might need *more* steps, not fewer — and that's okay.

- **Emotional co-regulation**. Your child needs your nervous system to help settle theirs. That might mean lying with them longer, using rhythmic touch, or narrating your own calm: "Let's take a deep breath together. My body is getting sleepy."

- **Clear but kind limit-setting**. "I won't leave the room until you're calm" is different from "Go to sleep, or I'm done."

- **Validation of experience**. Instead of "You're fine, it's bedtime," try "Your body feels too busy to sleep right now. Let's find a way to help it settle."

Case Story: Luca and the 17-Item Bedtime Checklist

Luca was five, with a sensory processing profile and suspected ADHD. His parents, Naomi and Julian, were burnt out from the nightly negotiations. "He needs so many things — his shark toy, his diffuser, the green pillow, the pink blanket but *not touching his toes...* It's too much."

We built a visual bedtime checklist *with* Luca. Seventeen items. Yes, really.

But here's the twist: once Luca had ownership of his checklist and the power to "tick things off," the chaos calmed. Instead of endless stalling, he became the bedtime captain. He still needed lots of support, but the predictability soothed him.

Gentle structure doesn't mean no boundaries — it means boundaries that *work* for the child's brain.

Practical Tools for Supporting the Neurodivergent Sleeper

Here's a toolbox that can be adapted to suit your child's unique wiring:

- **Visual schedules**: Help reduce anxiety about what comes next.

- **Timers or countdowns**: Make transitions concrete.

- **Movement before bed**: Use jumping, stretching, or swinging to help regulate.

- **Weighted blankets or body socks**: Deep pressure input helps some kids settle.

- **Comfort objects with purpose**: Fidget toys, chew necklaces, a soft "compression" buddy.

- **Sensory-friendly lighting**: Dimmable lamps or coloured lights can make the environment more calming.

- **Noise options**: White noise, nature sounds, or even rhythmic music to support downregulation.

- **Parent-led narration**: Calm voiceovers help co-regulate: "Now we're brushing our teeth. That tickles a little. Next, we'll snuggle into the blankets."

Sleep routines for neurodivergent children may take longer. They may need more steps, more prep, more patience. That doesn't mean they're failing. It means they're working hard — in ways we might not be able to see.

When You Feel Like You've Tried Everything

Let's be honest: this is exhausting.

When you've tried five weighted blankets, three types of white noise, changed routines a dozen times, and your child is *still* up at 10:30 p.m. building Lego towers, you start to feel like you're the problem. You're not.

Sometimes, the most powerful shift isn't a new product or strategy. It's giving yourself permission to let go of the "ideal" and focus on what *works* for your family.

Maybe your child won't fall asleep until 9 p.m., but they'll sleep through if you co-sleep. Maybe your routine doesn't look like anyone else's, but it works. That counts. That matters.

Case Story: Isla's Parents Found Peace at 10 p.m.

Isla was nine and had a dual diagnosis of autism and anxiety. Her bedtime had become a battleground of begging, screaming, and broken rules. Her parents were clinging to a 7:30 bedtime because that's what the sleep books — and their paediatrician — said she needed.

When we let that go and moved her bedtime later, everything changed. They still did the same wind-down routine — only now at 9:30. By 10:00, Isla was asleep, without the fight. Her body wasn't ready at 7:30, and pushing it led to distress. Once they stopped trying to make her fit the rule, she settled into a rhythm that worked.

There is no shame in adjusting your expectations. That's not giving up — it's tuning in.

Final Thoughts: Neurodivergence Is Not a Sleep Disorder

Your child is not broken. They don't need to be fixed. They need to be understood.

And yes, you need rest too. You're allowed to feel tired, frustrated, and over it. You're allowed to grieve the dream of easy sleep and still celebrate the small wins — like a bedtime that ended without tears, or a night where they only got up once.

Sleep support for neurodivergent children isn't about strict rules or fast fixes. It's about co-regulation, creativity, flexibility, and above all — compassion.

And if nobody's told you lately, you're doing an incredible job in a system that was never designed for your child.

Chapter 14

Separation Anxiety, Trauma, and Sleep

Sleep isn't just a biological process. For children, it's also an emotional one. To drift off, they need to feel safe enough to let go of the day and enter a vulnerable state where they're apart from you. This is why separation anxiety and trauma have such a profound impact on sleep: both strike at a child's sense of security, making the night feel like a risky place rather than a restful one.

In this chapter, we'll explore how separation anxiety and trauma show up in children's sleep, what's developmentally normal, and how you can gently support your child's regulation while still building healthy sleep patterns. Along the way, you'll meet families whose stories illustrate how different strategies can be applied in real life.

Separation Anxiety: Normal vs Overwhelming

Separation anxiety is a normal part of development. It usually appears around 8–10 months, peaks in toddlerhood, and can resurface during transitions — like starting school or moving house. At its core, it reflects healthy attachment: your child cares deeply about your presence and feels safest when you're nearby.

But for some children, separation anxiety is especially intense. Bedtime becomes a battleground, with clinginess, tears, and repeated calls for comfort. Night wakings often involve frantic crying until the parent returns.

Key signs it's overwhelming:

- Extreme distress when separated, even for short periods.

- Difficulty calming down even after reunions.

- Night wakings that feel more like panic than simple restlessness.

Case Illustration: Olivia (3 years old)

Olivia was a bright, curious preschooler who suddenly began refusing bedtime after her baby brother was born. She would cling to her mother's leg, sobbing if she tried to leave the room. At night, Olivia woke multiple times, rushing into her parents' bed.

Her behaviour wasn't "manipulation." It was a reflection of heightened separation anxiety — triggered by the transition of welcoming a new sibling. For Olivia, the night felt unsafe without her mother close by.

The family found progress with **camping out**. Olivia's mother stayed in the room at bedtime, gradually moving her chair further away over several weeks. At the same time, they built rituals of connection during the day — one-on-one play, special cuddles — so Olivia's "attachment tank" felt full. With time, her night fears eased.

When Trauma Shapes Sleep

Trauma — whether from medical procedures, family stress, grief, or frightening experiences — leaves an imprint on the nervous system. At night, when the world is dark and quiet, those imprints can resurface.

Trauma-related sleep disruptions often look different from garden-variety separation anxiety:

- Nightmares or night terrors

- Hypervigilance (difficulty falling asleep, startling awake easily)

- Resistance to being alone in the dark

- Re-enactment themes in play or dreams

Children who've experienced trauma may not simply "grow out of" these patterns without extra support. They need parents who respond with safety, predictability, and gentle reassurance.

Case Illustration: Ethan (6 years old)

Ethan had been in a car accident with his family. Although physically unharmed, he developed intense nighttime fears. He refused to sleep alone, woke screaming from nightmares, and insisted on keeping all the lights on.

His parents created a **trauma-informed sleep plan**:

- They introduced a nightlight and calming bedtime routine that emphasised safety (reading the same comforting story each night).

- They validated Ethan's fears instead of dismissing them: "It was scary, wasn't it? You're safe now, and we're here."

- They gradually encouraged independent sleep by first staying until he was drowsy, then stepping out for short intervals, always returning as promised.

Progress was slow, but Ethan eventually began sleeping more peacefully. What mattered most was that his parents met his fear with calm presence, not pressure to "be brave."

Practical Strategies for Parents

Whether your child is facing separation anxiety or trauma-related sleep struggles, the core principles are similar:

1. **Connection First**
   Fill your child's "attachment tank" during the day. One-on-one time, play, and physical affection go a long way toward easing night fears.

2. **Predictability and Rituals**
   Use the same bedtime routine each night. Familiar steps (bath, story, cuddle, prayer) create safety cues for the brain.

3. **Gradual Transitions**
   Don't expect instant independence. Start with presence — sitting nearby, holding a hand — then slowly reduce involvement as your child feels safe.

4. **Validate, Don't Dismiss**
   Avoid phrases like "There's nothing to be scared of." Instead, acknowledge the feeling: "I know you feel worried. I'm right here with you." Validation

calms the nervous system.

5. **Watch for Red Flags**
   If sleep struggles are severe, persistent, or linked to trauma that overwhelms daily life, professional support may be needed. Trauma-informed therapy can make a world of difference.

Even when you've found a rhythm that works, children's sleep can still take unexpected turns. Nightmares, night terrors, sleepwalking, and sudden regressions are all part of the sleep landscape at different ages. These episodes can feel alarming for parents — and exhausting — but most of the time, they are normal developmental events rather than signs of something "wrong."

This chapter will give you a quick guide to recognising what's happening and how to respond in ways that keep your child feeling safe.

Nightmares

Nightmares are frightening dreams that wake a child fully. They often appear between ages 3 and 6, when imagination is vivid and fears are common.

How to respond:

- Offer comfort and reassurance. Sit with your child until they're calm.

- Avoid dismissing fears ("It's just a dream"). Instead, acknowledge them: "That was scary, wasn't it? You're safe now."

- A nightlight, comfort toy, or predictable bedtime story can help reduce anxiety.

Nightmares can increase during times of stress, big transitions, or after exposure to frightening media.

Night Terrors

Night terrors look dramatic but are very different from nightmares. A child may scream, thrash, or appear terrified, but they are not fully awake and often don't remember it in the morning.

They usually occur in the first third of the night, during deep non-REM sleep.

How to respond:

- Stay calm. Your child is not aware in the same way as during a nightmare.

- Ensure safety (keep them from falling out of bed or hurting themselves).

- Avoid trying to wake them — it often prolongs the episode.

- Know that most children outgrow night terrors with time.

Other Common Disruptions

- **Sleepwalking**: Occurs in deep sleep, usually in school-aged children. Ensure the environment is safe (locks on doors, clear floors).

- **Bedtime fears**: Monsters, the dark, or being alone are common themes. Use validation, rituals, and comfort items rather than endless negotiations.

- **Sleep regressions**: Illness, travel, or developmental leaps can temporarily disrupt sleep. Respond with extra comfort when needed, then gently guide back to your usual routine once the disruption passes.

When to Seek Extra Help

Most of these disruptions are harmless and resolve with time. But seek professional advice if:

- Sleep problems are persistent and severely affecting daytime behaviour.

- Night terrors or sleepwalking put your child at risk of injury.

- Nightmares are frequent and tied to signs of trauma or ongoing anxiety.

Sleep isn't always smooth sailing, even in the most consistent homes. By understanding the difference between normal disruptions and problems needing extra help, you can respond calmly and compassionately. Your calm presence — whether during a nightmare cuddle or a middle-of-the-night reassurance — is what turns a scary night into a safe one.

Chapter 15

Your Attachment-Friendly Sleep Plan

By now, you've travelled through the world of sleep with me — from understanding how attachment shapes nighttime rhythms, to exploring the many behavioural tools available, to looking at special situations like separation anxiety, trauma, and neurodivergence.

If you've made it this far, you know something very important: there is no one-size-fits-all "solution." What matters most is building a sleep plan that feels right for your child, your values, and your family's wellbeing.

This chapter will help you bring all the pieces together into something practical — a personalised, attachment-friendly sleep plan.

Step 1: Anchor Yourself in Your Values

Before deciding *how* to change sleep, ask yourself:

- What matters most to me at night — speed, gentleness, consistency, or flexibility?

- How comfortable am I with crying, and how does that affect my tolerance for different methods?

- What rhythms or rituals feel sacred to our family?

When you're anchored in your values, you're less likely to second-guess yourself or feel pressured by conflicting advice.

Step 2: Know Your Child's Temperament

Temperament is the invisible hand that shapes how sleep strategies play out. Some children are naturally adaptable, while others are intense, sensitive, or slow to warm up.

- **Easy-going children** often tolerate structured approaches like controlled comforting.

- **Sensitive or anxious children** usually need gentler, presence-based strategies.

- **Intense kids** benefit from firm limits, but also lots of emotional co-regulation.

Remember: it's not about whether a method "works" in theory, but whether it fits *your child*.

Step 3: Pick Your Starting Rung on the Ladder

Think back to the "Ladder of Support." At the bottom are high-support strategies (feeding, rocking, lying beside). At the top is independent sleep.

Ask yourself:

- Where are we right now on this ladder?

- What's the next gentle step up we could try?

You don't need to leap from the bottom to the top in one night. Small steps, repeated consistently, add up.

Step 4: Build a Predictable Routine

Whatever approach you use, children need rhythm. Create a bedtime sequence that's the same every night — bath, pyjamas, story, prayer, cuddle, lights out. The predictability is what signals "safe sleep time" to the brain.

If your child struggles with transitions, use visual cues (like a picture chart) or simple verbal countdowns ("five more minutes of play, then bath").

Step 5: Expect Ups and Downs

Progress is rarely linear. Even after success, illness, travel, developmental leaps, or stress can bring sleep disruptions. That doesn't mean you've failed — it's just part of the process.

Use the ladder flexibly: sometimes you climb up, sometimes you climb back down. What matters is that you keep the overall direction steady.

Case Illustration: Two Families, Two Plans

The Harrisons had a 9-month-old who needed rocking to sleep every night. They felt okay with some crying but wanted to stay nearby. They chose **camping out**, starting beside the cot and gradually moving away. Within three weeks, their baby was settling independently with only brief protest.

The Lopez family had a 2-year-old with high anxiety. They couldn't tolerate controlled crying and knew their child needed closeness. They created a **gentle ladder plan**: first lying beside her, then sitting up, then sitting near the door. It took longer, but the process felt aligned with their values and their child's sensitivity.

Both families found success — not because they used the same method, but because they chose what fit them best.

Step 6: Protect Emotional Safety

Whatever plan you choose, hold onto this principle: sleep change should never come at the cost of emotional safety. That means:

- Responding with warmth, even if you're setting limits.

- Never leaving your child in prolonged distress without reassurance.

- Letting your child know that bedtime doesn't mean abandonment.

When emotional safety is protected, children don't just learn how to sleep — they also learn that relationships are safe, predictable, and trustworthy.

A Final Word of Encouragement

If you've ever lain awake at night, listening to your child cry, wondering if you're doing the right thing — you are not alone. Parents everywhere wrestle with these same questions.

There is no perfect plan, only the plan that feels right for your family. You don't have to break your bond to improve sleep. In fact, when you approach sleep with both structure and sensitivity, you strengthen it.

So take a breath. Trust that small, consistent steps will lead to progress. Celebrate the wins along the way — even if it's just one less waking, or a bedtime that runs more smoothly.

And above all, remember this: **your presence is the most powerful sleep aid your child will ever know.**

My Attachment-Friendly Sleep Plan

(Use this template to create a plan that fits your child, your values, and your family. Remember: this isn't about perfection — it's about finding the next gentle step forward.)

Step 1: My Values

What matters most to me when it comes to sleep?
- ☐ Gentleness
- ☐ Structure
- ☐ Flexibility
- ☐ Quick progress
- ☐ Emotional connection
- ☐ Other: _____

Step 2: My Child's Temperament

How would I describe my child?
- ☐ Easy-going / adaptable
- ☐ Sensitive / anxious
- ☐ Intense / strong-willed
- ☐ Slow to warm up

Notes:

_____

_____

_____

Step 3: Our Current Sleep Pattern

Bedtime routine:

_____

How my child currently falls asleep:

_____

Number of night wakings:

_____

How we usually respond at night:

_____

_____

Step 4: Where We Are on the Ladder of Support

(Current rung)
- ☐ Feeding to sleep
- ☐ Rocking/holding to sleep
- ☐ Parent lying beside child
- ☐ Parent sitting in room
- ☐ Parent checking in at intervals
- ☐ Independent sleep

Step 5: Our Next Gentle Step

What is the next step up the ladder we're aiming for?

_____

How we'll introduce it:

_____

_____

Step 6: Our Bedtime Routine

Step 1: _____

Step 2: _____

Step 3: _____

Step 4: _____

Step 5: _____

Step 7: Comfort Tools

What helps my child feel safe? (e.g., nightlight, lovey, prayer, music)

_____

_____

Step 8: How We'll Respond to Night Wakings

If my child wakes, we will:
- ☐ Offer comfort in bed
- ☐ Sit beside the cot/bed
- ☐ Use brief verbal reassurance
- ☐ Re-settle with feeding/cuddling
- ☐ Other: _____

Step 9: How We'll Care for Ourselves as Parents

What helps me stay calm and consistent at night?

Who can I ask for support if I feel stuck?

_____

_____

Step 10: Our Review Point

We will try this plan consistently for:
☐ 3 nights ☐ 1 week ☐ 2 weeks ☐ Other:
_____

On review, we'll adjust by:

_____

_____

Want personalised support? Our **Institute of Sensitive Sleep Consulting** has trained sleep consultants far and wide, so why not reach out to a caring professional who deeply understands our attachment approach to take an outside-in look and walk with you. Google Sensitive Sleep Consultant in your country to find a trained consultant or visit www.instituteofsensitivesleep.com to learn more about us.

Afterword

As I write these final words, I'm thinking not just of sleep, but of what sleep represents. Every bedtime is a moment of surrender — for our children and, in many ways, for us as parents. It's a letting go of control, a trust that safety will hold through the night, and a reminder that rest is just as important as all the "doing" we fill our days with.

If you've walked through this book, you've probably discovered what I've discovered many times in my own journey as a parent, a sleep consultant, and a therapist: there are no shortcuts, no magic fixes, and no single "right" way. There are just families, each unique, learning to balance love and limits, patience and persistence, presence and independence.

When I look back on my years supporting parents, I can tell you this with confidence: you don't have to choose between healthy sleep and emotional connection. In fact, the two thrive together. When a child feels safe, they sleep more soundly. And when a parent feels secure in their approach, the whole family rests easier.

So if you've ever doubted yourself in the quiet hours of the night, please hear this: you are not failing. You are showing up. You are learning, adjusting, and trying again — and that is the heart of good parenting.

As you put down this book and look ahead, may you carry with you the reassurance that progress is always possible, and that attachment-friendly sleep is not just about nights — it's about nurturing trust that lasts a lifetime.

From one parent to another, and from my heart to yours: You've got this. And you're not alone.

Rest well.

— *Kel*

INSTITUTE OF SENSITIVE
SLEEP CONSULTING
10 YEAR ANNIVERSARY

More titles from this publisher can be ordered at www.instituteofsensitivesleep.com or www.erinnah.org

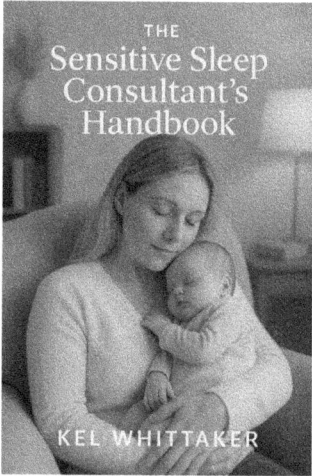

THE
Sensitive Sleep
Consultant's
Handbook

KEL WHITTAKER

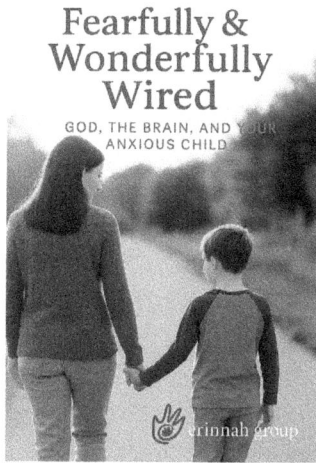

Fearfully &
Wonderfully
Wired

GOD, THE BRAIN, AND YOUR
ANXIOUS CHILD

erinnah group

www.ingramcontent.com/pod-product-compliance
Lightning Source LLC
Chambersburg PA
CBHW051816090426
42736CB00011B/1514